KÖNEMANN

© 2015 for this edition: koenemann.com GmbH
Distributed in cooperation with Frechmann Kolón GmbH

www.koenemann.com
www.frechmann.com

Published in the United States in 2016 by:

Skyhorse Publishing
307 West 36th Street, 11th Floor
New York, NY 10018, USA
T: +1 212 643 6816

info@skyhorsepublishing.com
www.skyhorsepublishing.com

Editorial project: LOFT Publications
Barcelona, Spain
Tel.: +34 932 688 088
Fax: +34 932 687 073
loft@loftpublications.com
www.loftpublications.com

Editorial coordinator: Aitana Lleonart Triquell
Assistant to editorial coordination: Ana Marques
Edition and texts: Francesc Zamora Mola
Editor's assistant: Yuri Caravaca Gallardo
Graphic edition: Cristina Paredes Benítez
Art director: Mireia Casanovas Soley
Design and layout coordination: Claudia Martínez Alonso
Layout: Cristina Simó Perales
Layout assistant: Paco Ortiz García
Translations: Cillero & de Motta

ISBN 978-3-86407-295-6 (GB)
ISBN 978-3-86407-293-2 (D)
ISBN 978-3-86407-294-9 (E)
ISBN 978-1-5107-0455-8 (Skyhorse, USA)

Printed in Spain

For a long time now, the emphasis in innovative residential architecture has rested on the challenge of designing homes in urban environments. The focus in the design of country homes has been in preservation, conversion and renovation of existing buildings. *Modern Country Homes* explores how architects today strive to reinvent the country house and develop a new rural architecture, rather than simply remodeling or recreating traditional forms and techniques. In some countries, building regulations in the countryside have been changed to allow new constructions that reflect the highest standards of contemporary architecture.

In addition to some case studies of remodels, many houses shown in this book are part of a contemporary architectural trend: a radical change in conceiving the residential architecture of the countryside derived from the increasing number of families who have moved to the country to escape from the stresses of urban life. This has resulted in the transfer of an urban design consciousness out of the cities and into rugged natural environments. Climate is undoubtedly one of the elements to consider when analyzing the determinants of architecture in the mountains. The entire process, from design to the choice of materials is influenced by specific weather conditions. These factors include sunlight, humidity and temperature variations, snow and wind. Location and orientation of buildings are also crucial considerations for a house in the country. How to overcome the slope of the plot, the existing vegetation or the lack of municipal water supply are some additional difficulties in designing such homes. Nonetheless, we could define these homes as simple and practical, but, most importantly, as a type of construction aimed at integration into the landscape.

Modern Country Homes is an illustrated book filled with what is new in country house design. The houses included in the book are uncompromisingly modern and, at the same time, respectful of the landscape. They offer a breath of fresh air that evolves from the traditional rural home, with pitched and mansard roofs organized around a hearth. They are more complex and sometimes of a grander scale, but they broaden the conceptualization of a relaxed and user-friendly style. Selected on the basis of their innovation in the field, these houses make *Modern Country Homes* a highly useful sourcebook for architects, designers, and students of architecture who are interested in the aesthetically groundbreaking and often ecologically conscious way of living represented by today's new country houses.

Depuis longtemps maintenant, les défis relatifs à la conception de foyers en milieu urbain occupent une place centrale dans l'architecture résidentielle contemporaine. L'agencement des maisons de campagne repose quant à lui davantage sur la préservation, la conservation et la rénovation de bâtiments existants. *Maisons de campagne contemporaines* explore les efforts déployés par les architectes pour réinventer la maison de campagne et développer une nouvelle architecture allant plus loin que le simple remodelage des formes et techniques traditionnelles. Dans certains pays, les règlementations de la construction en milieu rural ont évolué et permettent aujourd'hui l'élaboration de bâtiments s'élevant aux standards les plus hauts de l'architecture contemporaine.

Outre quelques études de cas de remodelages, bon nombre des maisons présentées ici reflètent la tendance architecturale contemporaine : un changement radical dans la conception des maisons de campagne, qui s'explique par le nombre croissant de familles s'installant en milieu rural pour fuir le stress de la ville. Le phénomène s'est traduit par le transfert des concepts de design urbains depuis la ville vers les environnements naturels rustiques. Le climat constitue bien évidemment l'un des éléments à prendre en compte lors de l'analyse des déterminants de l'architecture en montagne. L'intégralité du processus, du dessin au choix des matériaux, est influencée par des conditions climatiques spécifiques. Ces facteurs comprennent notamment l'ensoleillement, l'humidité, les variations de température, la neige et le vent. L'emplacement et l'orientation des bâtiments sont également des caractéristiques fondamentales pour une maison en milieu rural. La réalisation de ce genre de maisons suppose certaines difficultés supplémentaires à surmonter, comme par exemple un terrain en pente, une végétation abondante ou encore une absence de raccordement à l'eau de ville. Néanmoins, ces foyers peuvent être définis comme simples et fonctionnels mais également, plus important encore, comme un type de constructions visant à s'intégrer dans le paysage.

Maisons de campagne contemporaines est un livre illustré qui rend compte d'un nombre considérable de nouveautés en matière de design de maisons de campagne. Les maisons présentées ici sont indéniablement modernes tout en demeurant respectueuses de leur environnement. Elles représentent une bouffée d'air frais s'inspirant des maisons rurales traditionnelles, avec des toits à deux pans et des plafonds mansardés, entièrement agencées autour d'une cheminée. Elles sont plus complexes et parfois de plus grande échelle, mais elles représentent avant tout la conceptualisation étendue d'un style décontracté et convivial. Choisies selon leur innovation en la matière, ces maisons font de ce livre un ouvrage de référence pour les architectes, designers et étudiants en architecture intéressés par les esthétiques avant-gardistes et les modes de vie écologiques propres aux nouvelles maisons de campagne de notre époque.

Über lange Zeit hinweg lag der Schwerpunkt innovativer Wohnungsbauarchitektur in der Herausforderung, Häuser in Stadtgebieten zu entwerfen. Beim Entwurf von Landhäusern konzentrierte sich das Interesse auf Erhaltung, Umwandlung und Umbau bestehender Häuser. *Moderne & Exklusive Landhäuser* untersucht das aktuelle Bestreben der Architekten, Landhäuser neu zu erfinden und eine neue Landhausarchitektur zu entwickeln, und sich auf diese Art nicht auf Umbau und Nachbildung traditioneller Formen und Techniken zu begrenzen. In einigen Ländern wurden die Bauvorschriften auf dem Land in dem Sinne geändert, dass neue Bauten die anspruchsvolleren Kriterien der zeitgenössischen Architektur widerspiegeln können.

Neben einigen Beispielen für Umbauten sind die in diesem Buch dargestellten Häuser Teil eines zeitgenössischen architektonischen Trends: Der radikale Wechsel in der Vorstellung der Landhausarchitektur, der sich daraus ableitet, dass immer mehr Familien aufs Land ziehen, um dem hektischen Leben in der Stadt zu entfliehen. Als Folge daraus ist eine Umstellung im Bewusstsein des städtischen Entwurfs in Richtung rustikalerer natürlicher Umgebungen erfolgt. Das Klima ist zweifellos eines der Elemente, das bei der Untersuchung der Bedingungen der Architektur in den Bergen berücksichtigt werden muss. Der gesamte Ablauf vom Entwurf bis zur Auswahl des Baumaterials hängt von konkreten Wetterbedingungen oder Faktoren wie Tageslicht, Feuchtigkeit, Temperaturschwankungen, Schnee und Wind ab. Standort und Ausrichtung der Gebäude sind bei Landhäusern auch ausschlaggebende Faktoren, die zu berücksichtigen sind. Geländeneigungen, vorhandene Vegetation oder fehlende kommunale Wasserversorgung sind zusätzliche Probleme, die zum Entwurf dieser Häuser hinzukommen. Diese wiederum können als einfach und praktisch und - vielleicht noch wichtiger - als Bauten angesehen werden, die sich in die Landschaft integrieren sollen.

Moderne & Exklusive Landhäuser ist ein illustriertes Buch voller Neuheiten beim Landhausentwurf. Die in diesem Buch dargestellten Häuser sind absolut modern und gleichzeitig respektvoll gegenüber der Landschaft. Sie bieten frischen Wind, indem sie eine Weiterentwicklung vom traditionellen Landhaus mit Schrägdächern und Dachluken um einen Schornstein herum ermöglicht haben. In einigen Fällen sind sie komplexer und stellen beeindruckende Abmessungen dar, obwohl sie die Vorstellung eines entspannteren und einfachen Stils ausführen. Sie wurden aufgrund ihrer Innovation in der Branche ausgewählt und machen *Moderne & Exklusive Landhäuser* zu einem sehr nützlichen Nachschlagewerk für Architekten, Designer und Architekturstudenten, die an einem innovativen Lebensstil aus ästhetischem und oftmals auch umweltfreundlichem Gesichtspunkt der heutigen Landhäuser interessiert sind.

Lange tijd lag bij innovatieve residentiële architectuur de nadruk op de uitdaging van het ontwerpen van woningen in stedelijke gebieden. Bij het ontwerpen van huizen op het platteland lag het accent op het behouden, omvormen en renoveren van bestaande gebouwen. *Moderne Landhuizen* onderzoekt hoe architecten zich vandaag de dag inspannen om het landhuis opnieuw uit te vinden en om een nieuwe rurale architectuur tot ontwikkeling te brengen, in plaats van het simpelweg omvormen of herscheppen van traditionele vormen en technieken. In sommige landen zijn de bouwvoorschriften op het platteland veranderd, zodat nieuwe bouwwerken zijn toegestaan die blijk kunnen geven van de hoge criteria van eigentijdse architectuur.

Naast enkele voorbeelden van renovaties, maken vele in dit boek getoonde woningen deel uit van een hedendaagse architectuurtrend: een radicale verandering in het idee van residentiële architectuur op het platteland, die voortvloeit uit het toenemende aantal gezinnen dat naar het platteland verhuist om te ontsnappen aan de stress van het stadsleven. Dit heeft een ommekeer teweeg gebracht in het bewustzijn op het gebied van stedelijk ontwerp, vanuit de steden naar meer landelijke omgevingen. Het klimaat is ongetwijfeld een van de elementen om rekening mee te houden bij het analyseren van de bepalende factoren van architectuur in de bergen. Het gehele proces, van het ontwerp tot aan de materiaalkeuze, wordt beïnvloed door specifieke weersomstandigheden. Deze factoren zijn onder meer zonlicht, vochtigheid en temperatuurschommelingen, sneeuw en wind. De locatie en oriëntatie van gebouwen zijn eveneens elementen om in gedachten te houden bij een huis op het platteland. De manier waarop de helling van de kavel moet worden overbrugd, de bestaande begroeiing of het gebrek aan een gemeentelijke watervoorziening zijn enkele bijkomende moeilijkheden die komen kijken bij het ontwerpen van dergelijke huizen. Wij kunnen deze woningen echter omschrijven als simpel en praktisch en bovendien, en dat is het belangrijkste, als bouwwerken met de bedoeling om in het landschap te integreren.

Moderne Landhuizen is een geïllustreerd boek, vol met nieuwigheden op het gebied van het ontwerp van landhuizen. De huizen die in dit boek aan bod komen zijn onherroepelijk modern en tegelijkertijd respectvol met het landschap. Ze bieden een vleugje frisse lucht: ze maken het mogelijk om het traditionele landhuis met schuin aflopend dak en ingericht rond een haard, tot ontwikkeling te brengen. Ze zijn complexer en in sommige gevallen groter, maar gaan uit van het idee van een relaxte en gebruiksvriendelijke stijl. Deze huizen, die geselecteerd zijn op grond van hun innovatie binnen het werkgebied, maken van *Moderne Landhuizen* een zeer bruikbaar naslagwerk voor architecten, ontwerpers en bouwkundestudenten met belangstelling voor deze esthetische, baanbrekende en vaak milieuvriendelijke manier van wonen, die vertegenwoordigd wordt door de nieuwe landhuizen van vandaag de dag.

Durante mucho tiempo, el énfasis de la arquitectura residencial innovadora se basó en el reto de diseñar casas en entornos urbanos. Para el diseño de casas de campo, el interés se centró en la conservación, transformación y renovación de viviendas existentes. *Casas de campo modernas* explora la lucha actual de los arquitectos para reinventar la casa de campo y desarrollar una nueva arquitectura rural, y así no limitarse a reformar o recrear las formas y técnicas tradicionales. En algunos países se han modificado las normativas de construcción en el campo para que las nuevas edificaciones puedan reflejar los criterios más elevados de la arquitectura contemporánea.

Además de algunos ejemplos de reformas, muchas de las casas mostradas en este libro forman parte de una tendencia arquitectónica contemporánea: el cambio radical en la idea de la arquitectura residencial de campo, derivado del número cada vez mayor de familias que se trasladan a entornos rurales para escapar del estrés de la vida en la ciudad. Como consecuencia, se ha producido un cambio de conciencia de diseño urbano de las ciudades a los entornos naturales más rústicos. El clima, sin duda, es uno de los elementos que deben considerarse al analizar los condicionantes de la arquitectura en las montañas. Todo el proceso, desde el diseño hasta la elección de los materiales, depende de las condiciones meteorológicas concretas, de factores como la luz natural, la humedad, las variaciones de temperatura, la nieve y el viento. La ubicación y la orientación de los edificios también son elementos cruciales que deben tenerse en cuenta en una casa de campo. Cómo superar la inclinación del terreno, la vegetación existente o la falta de suministro municipal de agua son dificultades que se añaden al diseño de estas casas que, no obstante, podríamos definir como sencillas y prácticas, y lo que es más importante, como construcciones destinadas a integrarse en el paisaje.

Casas de campo modernas es un libro ilustrado repleto de novedades en el diseño de casas de campo. Las casas recogidas en el libro son irremediablemente modernas y, al mismo tiempo, respetuosas con el paisaje. Ofrecen un soplo de aire fresco: han permitido evolucionar de la casa rural tradicional con techos inclinados y abuhardillados, organizada en torno a una chimenea. Son más complejas y, en ocasiones, presentan unas dimensiones más imponentes, aunque desarrollan la idea de un estilo relajado y sencillo. Seleccionadas por su innovación en el ámbito, estas casas hacen de *Casas de campo modernas* un libro de consulta muy útil para arquitectos, diseñadores y estudiantes de arquitectura interesados en un estilo de vida innovador desde un punto de vista estético, y con frecuencia ecológico, representado por las actuales casas de campo.

Da molto tempo ormai l'enfasi della nuova architettura residenziale si concentra sulla sfida data dalla progettazione di nuclei abitativi all'interno di contesti urbani. L'attenzione nella progettazione di case rurali è stata rivolta alla conservazione, conversione e ristrutturazione di edifici esistenti. *Moderne case di campagna* mostra come gli architetti oggi lavorino per reinventare la casa di campagna e sviluppare una nuova architettura rurale, piuttosto che per ristrutturare o ricreare semplicemente forme e tecniche tradizionali. In alcuni paesi le normative edilizie per gli ambienti rurali sono cambiate per consentire la realizzazione di nuove strutture che riflettano gli standard elevati dell'architettura contemporanea.

Oltre ad alcuni esempi di ristrutturazioni, molte case illustrate in questo libro testimoniano la tendenza che caratterizza l'architettura contemporanea: un cambiamento radicale nel modo di concepire l'architettura residenziale rurale, derivante dall'aumento nel numero di famiglie che si trasferiscono in campagna per fuggire dallo stress della vita cittadina. Questo ha portato al trasferimento della coscienza progettuale urbana dalla città a contesti naturali rurali. Il clima è senza dubbio uno degli elementi da prendere in considerazione nell'analisi degli aspetti che determinano l'architettura montana. L'intero processo, dalla progettazione alla scelta dei materiali, è influenzato da specifiche condizioni ambientali. Tali fattori comprendono la luce solare, l'umidità e le variazioni di temperatura, la neve e il vento. Anche la posizione e l'orientamento degli edifici sono fattori cruciali di cui tenere conto per una casa di campagna. Come risolvere la presenza di un dislivello, la vegetazione esistente o la mancanza di fornitura idrica pubblica sono alcune delle difficoltà aggiuntive nella progettazione di questo tipo di abitazioni. Tuttavia possiamo definire queste case semplici e funzionali, ma soprattutto, un tipo di edificio che mira a integrarsi con l'ambiente circostante.

Moderne case di campagna è un libro illustrato che raccoglie le novità sulla progettazione delle case di campagna. Le abitazioni illustrate nel libro non rinunciano alla modernità ma, nello stesso tempo, rispettano il paesaggio. Offrono uno sguardo nuovo e fresco rispetto al concetto tradizionale di casa rurale, con tetti a mansarda e a spiovente organizzati intorno a un nucleo centrale. Sono soluzioni più complesse e talvolta di grande scala, ma ampiano il concetto di stile rilassato e funzionale. Selezionate in base al loro grado di innovazione nel settore, queste case rendono *Moderne case di campagna* un libro molto utile per architetti, designer e studenti di architettura interessati a un modo di vivere esteticamente innovativo e spesso ecologicamente consapevole, rappresentato dalle nuove case rurali.

Já há muito tempo que a ênfase na inovação da arquitectura residencial repousa no desafio do desenho de casas em ambientes urbanos. O ponto central no desenho de casas de campo tem sido a preservação, conservação e renovação de edifícios existentes. *Casas de Campo Modernas* explora como os arquitectos hoje em dia se esforçam por reinventar a casa de campo e desenvolvem uma nova arquitectura rural, em vez de uma simples remodelação ou recriação de técnicas e formas tradicionais. Em alguns países, as normas de construção referentes ao campo foram alteradas para permitir novas construções que reflictam os mais elevados *standards* da arquitectura contemporânea.

Para além alguns estudos de casos de remodelações, muitas casas exibidas neste livro são parte de uma tendência da arquitectura contemporânea: uma mudança radical na concepção da arquitectura residencial de campo derivada do aumento do número de famílias que se moveram para o campo para fugir ao *stress* da vida urbana. Tal resultou na transferência de uma consciência de desenho urbano fora das cidades e dentro de ambientes naturais rigorosos. O clima é indubitavelmente um dos elementos a considerar quando se analisa as determinantes da arquitectura nas montanhas. Todo o processo, desde o desenho à escolha dos materiais é influenciado pelas condições de tempo específicas. Estes factores incluem variações de temperatura, humidade e luz solar, neve e vento. A localização e orientação dos edifícios são também considerações cruciais para uma casa no campo. Como superar o declive do terreno, a vegetação existente ou a falta de fornecimento de água municipal são algumas das dificuldades adicionais no desenho destas casas. Contudo, podemos definir estas casas como simples e práticas, mas o mais importante, como um tipo de construção dirigidas para a integração no meio ambiente.

Casas de Campo Modernas é um livro ilustrado que contém tudo o que é novidade no desenho de casas de campo. As casas incluídas no livro são incondicionalmente modernas e, ao mesmo tempo, respeitam a paisagem. Oferecem uma lufada de ar fresco que evolui da tradicional casa de campo com telhados de duas águas e mansardas organizadas em volta de um coração. Elas são mais complexas e por vezes de uma escala maior, mas alargam a conceptualização de um estilo relaxado e de fácil utilização. Seleccionadas em base da sua inovação no campo, estas casas fazem de *Casas de Campo Modernas* um livro de referência extremamente útil para arquitectos, desenhadores, e estudantes de arquitectura interessados na forma de viver estética, inovadora e muitas vezes ecologicamente consciente, representada pelas casas de campo de hoje em dia.

Tyngdpunkten inom innovativ bostadsarkitektur har under lång tid nu vilat på utmaningen att rita bostäder i stadsmiljö. Vad gäller ritning av hus på landet har fokus legat inom bevaring, ombyggnad och renovering av befintliga byggnader. *Moderna hus på landet* utforskar hur arkitekter idag strävar efter att återuppfinna huset på landet och att utveckla en ny landsbygdsarkitektur snarare än att bara bygga om eller återskapa traditionella former och tekniker. I en del länder har byggreglerna på landet ändrats för att tillåta nya konstruktioner där de högsta standarderna i samtida arkitektur reflekteras.

Förutom några fallstudier rörande ombyggnader utgör många av husen som visas i denna bok en del av en modern arkitektonisk trend: en radikal förändring i begreppet bostadsarkitektur på landsbygden, vilken härrör från det ökande antalet familjer som har flyttat till landet för att fly stadslivets stress. Detta har resulterat i att en medvetenhet inom urban design har flyttat från städerna ut till tuffa, naturliga miljöer. Ett av elementen att ha i åtanke i analysen av de avgörande faktorerna för arkitektur i bergen är utan tvekan klimatet. Hela processen, från design till valet av material, påverkas av bestämda väderförhållanden. Dessa förhållanden innefattar solljus, fuktighet och temperaturvariationer, snö och vind. Byggnadernas plats och orientering är också viktiga överväganden för ett hus på landet. Hur man övervinner tomtens lutning, den befintliga växtligheten eller bristen på kommunal vattenförsörjning är några av de extra svårigheter man möter i utformningen av sådana hem. Det oaktat skulle vi kunna definiera dessa hem som enkla och praktiska men framförallt som en typ av konstruktion som syftar till integration i landskapet.

Moderna hus på landet är en illustrerad bok fylld med allt nytt inom design av hus på landet. Husen som är med i boken är kompromisslöst moderna och samtidigt respektfulla mot landskapet. De ger en fläkt av frisk luft som härleder till det traditionella landsbygdshemmet med sina sluttande tak och mansardtak arrangerade kring hemmets härd. De är mer komplexa och ibland av större skala men de breddar konceptualiseringen av en avslappnad och användarvänlig stil. Dessa hus har valts ut på grundval av sin innovation inom området och gör *Moderna hus på landet* till en mycket användbar källbok för arkitekter, designers och studenter inom arkitektur som är intresserade av det estetiskt banbrytande och ofta ekologiskt medvetna sättet att leva som representeras av dagens nya landsbygdshus.

APTOS RETREAT

CCS Architecture
Aptos, CA, USA
© Paul Dyer

The layout of the buildings reflects a functional screen: on one side, the areas of daily activity and relaxation in the main house, with their recovered wood façade and the cement, wood, stone and steel interior, and on the other, the recreational areas of the barn, with its rusty-steel exterior, and other separated dwellings.

La disposition des édifices reflète une séparation fontionnelle : d'une part, les zones d'activité quotidienne et de repos, intégrées au logement principal, avec une façade en bois de récupération et l'intérieur en béton, bois, pierre et acier ; d'autre part, les zones récréatives de la grange (extérieur en acier inoxydable) et autres annexes dispersées.

Die Anordnung der Gebäude zeigt eine funktionale Trennung: Auf einer Seite befinden sich die Bereiche der täglichen Aktivität und Erholung, die im Hauptgebäude mit dessen Fassade aus recyceltem Haus und dem Innenbereich aus Zement, Holz, Stein und Stahl bestehen. Auf der anderen Seite der Vergnügungsbereich der Scheune, mit ihrer Außenseite aus verrostetem Stahl und den weiteren getrennten Räumlichkeiten.

De manier waarop de gebouwen geplaatst zijn geeft blijk van een functionele selectie. Aan een kant zijn de zones waarin zich het dagelijkse leven afspeelt en de rustgedeeltes geïntegreerd in de hoofdwoning, met zijn gevel van gerecycled hout en cement, hout, steen in het interieur. Aan de andere kant liggen de recreatieve zones van de graanschuur —met geoxideerd staal aan de buitenkant— en de overige binnenruimtes verspreid.

La disposición de los edificios refleja una criba funcional: de un lado, las áreas de actividad cotidiana y reposo integradas en la casa principal, con su fachada de maderas recuperadas y su interior de cemento, madera, piedra y acero; del otro, las zonas recreativas del granero —con su exterior de acero oxidado— y demás habitáculos disgregados.

La disposizione degli edifici riflette un criterio funzionale: da un lato le aree di attività quotidiana e riposo integrate nella casa principale, con la sua facciata in legno recuperato e gli interni in cemento, legno, pietra e acciaio; dall'altro le zone dedicate alle attività ludiche del granaio - con la parte esterna in acciaio ossidato - e altri ambienti sparsi sul terreno.

A disposição dos edifícios reflecte um crivo funcional: de um lado as áreas de actividade quotidiana e repouso integradas na casa principal, com a sua fachada de madeiras recuperadas e o seu interior de cimento, madeira, pedra e aço; do outro, as zonas recreativas do celeiro —com o seu exterior de aço oxidado— e demais habitáculos desagregados.

Byggnadernas placering återspeglar ett funktionellt urval: å ena sidan utrymme för de dagliga aktiviteterna och vila integrerade i huvudbyggnaden, med sin fasad av återställt trä och insida av cement, och å andra sidan logens förströelseutrymmen, med rostigt stål utvändigt, samt övriga avdelade rum.

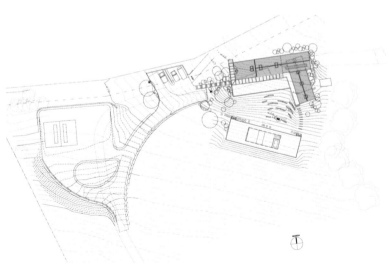

Site plan

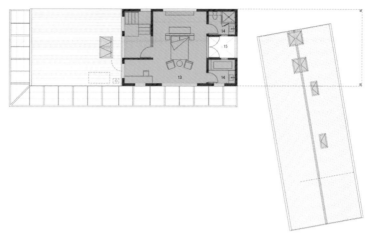

Second floor

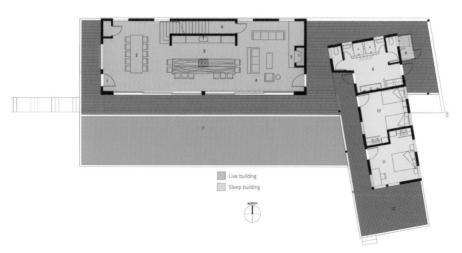

1. Entry
2. Dining room
3. Kitchen
4. Living room
5. Fireplace
6. Pantry
7. Lawn
8. Bath house
9. Outdoor shower
10. Bedroom
11. Bedroom
12. South deck
13. Master suite
14. Split bathroom
15. Open to below

Live building
Sleep building

NORTH

Ground floor

13

YUM YUM FARM

DeForest Architects
Iowa, IA, USA
© Farshid Assassi, Ben Benschneider

The picturesque appearance of this house, similar to an Amish farm with a pitched roof and individual porches as cantilevers, reveals an interior with modern principles of sustainability and functionality. Almost entirely constructed from recycled materials, the house boasts open-plan and versatile spaces.

Derrière l'apparence pittoresque de cette maison aux allures de ferme *Amish* – toit à deux pans et porches en saillies – se cache un intérieur conforme aux critères contemporains de durabilité et de fonctionnalité. Presque entièrement construite avec des matériaux recyclés, cette maison se compose d'espaces diaphanes et polyvalents.

Hinter dem malerischen Aussehen dieses Hauses im Stile eines *amish* Bauernhofs mit Satteldach und zwei Vorhallen als Auskragungen, steckt ein Innenraum, der moderne Kriterien wie Nachhaltigkeit und Funktionalität erfüllt. Es ist fast vollständig aus Recyclingmaterial erbaut und bietet leere wie auch Mehrzweckräume.

Onder de pittoreske verschijning van dit huis, met het stempel van een *Amish* boerderij – zadeldak dak met even zovele overdekte galerijen als uitstekende delen – wordt in het interieur voldaan aan de moderne criteria van duurzaamheid en functionaliteit. Het huis, dat bijna geheel is opgebouwd uit gerecyclede materialen, is een toonbeeld van lichte en polyvalente ruimtes.

Bajo la apariencia pintoresca de esta casa, con el marchamo de una granja *amish* –tejado a dos aguas con sendos porches a modo de voladizos–, late un interior rendido a modernos criterios de sostenibilidad y funcionalidad. Casi enteramente construida con materiales reciclados, la casa es un muestrario de espacios diáfanos y polivalentes.

Dietro l'apparenza pittoresca di questa casa, in tipico stile *Amish* – tetto a doppio spiovente con vari porticati con copertura sospesa – si sviluppa un ambiente interno che applica i moderni criteri di sostenibilità e funzionalità. Quasi interamente realizzata con materiali riciclati, la casa si compone di spazi luminosi e polivalenti.

Sob a aparência pitoresca desta casa, com o cunho de uma quinta *Amish* – telhado de duas águas com os seus respectivos alpendres tipo pala –, late um interior rendido aos modernos critérios de sustentabilidade e funcionalidade. Quase inteiramente construída com materiais reciclados, a casa é um mostruário de espaços diáfanos e polivalentes.

Under detta husets pittoreska utseende, med prägel från en *amishgård* och med sadeltak och enskilda verandor som utsprång, pulserar en interiör utformad med moderna principer för hållbarhet och funktionalitet. Huset som nästan uteslutande har byggts med återvunna material är en brokig samling av öppna och mångsidiga ytor.

WEEKEND HOUSE

Pokorny Architekti
Nosice, Slovakia
© Dano Veselsky

The role of wood both on the exterior – the pine-insulated panels – and in the interior – the larch tables – refers to the traditional Slovak cottages. Inside, the leisure areas – the sun deck above and bathing areas in the basement –, and the bedrooms revolve around a two story high living-dining room.

L'importance du bois tant à l'extérieur – panneaux isolants en pin – qu'à l'intérieur – étagères en cèdre – rappelle les maisons slovaques traditionnelles. À l'intérieur, les espaces de détente - solarium au-dessus et salle de bains en sous-sol - et les chambres sont agencés autour d'un salon-salle à manger sur deux étages.

Das Vorherrschen des Holzes sowohl außen – Isolierplatten aus Kiefernholz –, wie auch innen – Lärchentafeln – spielt auf die traditionellen slowakischen Landhäuser an. Innerhalb drehen sich die Entspannungsbereiche mit Solarium oben und Bäderbereich im Untergeschoss, wie auch die Schlafzimmer, um ein zwei Etagen hohes Wohn- und Esszimmer.

De centrale rol van hout, zowel buiten –isolerende grenenhouten panelen– als binnen –larikshouten bladen– verwijzen naar de traditionele Slowaakse landhuizen. Van binnen zijn de dagruimtes –solarium boven en badkamers in het souterrain– en de slaapkamers ingedeeld rond een salon en eetkamer van twee verdiepingen.

El protagonismo de la madera tanto en el exterior –paneles aislantes de pino– como en los interiores –tablas de alerce– alude a las tradicionales casas de campo eslovacas. Dentro, las zonas de asueto –solárium arriba y zona de baños en el sótano– y los dormitorios pivotan alrededor de un salón-comedor de dos plantas de altura.

Il protagonismo del legno sia all'esterno - pannelli isolanti di pino - che all'interno - tavole di larice - richiama le case tradizionali della campagna slovacca. All'interno, le zone relax - solarium al piano alto e zona bagni nel seminterrato--e le camere ruotano intorno a un salotto-tinello alto due piani.

O protagonismo da madeira tanto no exterior – painéis isolantes de pinho – como nos interiores – tábuas de alerce – alude às tradicionais casas de campo eslovacas. Dentro, as zonas de descanso – solário em cima e zona de banhos na cave – e os quartos rondam uma sala de jantar de pé direito duplo.

Huvudrollen som trä spelar såväl utomhus i isoleringspaneler av furu, som inomhus i plankor av lärk, anspelar på traditionella, slovakiska hus på landet. Inomhus finns platser för avkoppling med solarium där uppe och badutrymme i källaren, och sovrummen är belägna runt ett gemensamt matsal-vardagsrum på två våningar.

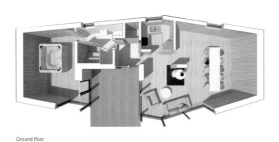

Ground floor

Second floor

INNFELD HOUSE

Dietrich + Untertrifaller Architekten
Schwarzenberger, Austria
© Ignacio Martínez

The building, subject to the landscape, reverses the conventional distribution: the transparency of the attic is reserved for common areas, the bedrooms are relegated to the basement. The exterior larch gives it a lightweight and breathable aspect. Inside, the brown walnut flooring makes the plaster walls and sallow tone of the woodwork stand out.

Le bâtiment, subordonné au paysage, inverse l'agencement traditionnel : la transparence du dernier étage est réservée aux espaces communs tandis que les chambres sont reléguées au sous-sol. Le cèdre extérieur apporte un aspect frais et léger. À l'intérieur, le sol brun noyer fait ressortir le crépi des murs et les tons olive de la menuiserie.

Das der Landschaft untergeordnete Gebäude kehrt die herkömmliche Aufteilung um: Die Attikatransparenz bleibt den Gemeinschaftsbereichen vorbehalten und die Schlafzimmer werden auf das Untergeschoss verbannt. Lärchenholz im Außenbereich verleiht dem Gebäude einen leichten und durchlässigen Eindruck. Innerhalb betont der braune Nussholzboden den Verputz der Wände und den gelbgrünen Ton der Tür- und Fensterrahmen.

Het gebouw, dat is onderworpen aan het landschap, keert de conventionele indeling om: de transparantie van de zolderverdieping is gereserveerd voor de gemeenschappelijke ruimtes; de slaapkamers zijn naar het souterrain verplaatst. Het larikshout aan de buitenkant geeft het huis een licht en vrij uiterlijk. Van binnen benadrukt het bruingrijze notenhout op de vloer het pleisterwerk van de muren en de olijfkleurige tint van de kozijnen.

El edificio, supeditado al paisaje, invierte la distribución convencional: la transparencia del ático se reserva a las áreas comunes; los dormitorios se relegan al sótano. El alerce exterior le otorga un aspecto liviano y transpirable. Dentro, el pardo nogal del suelo resalta el enlucido de las paredes y el tono cetrino de la carpintería.

L'edificio, subordinato al paesaggio, inverte la distribuzione convenzionale: la trasparenza dell'attico è riservata alle aree comuni, mentre le camere si trovano nel seminterrato. Il larice esterno trasmette leggerezza e traspirabilità. All'interno, lo scuro noce del pavimento mette in risalto l'intonaco delle pareti e il tono olivastro delle finiture in legno.

O edifício, subordinado à paisagem, inverte a distribuição convencional: a transparência do sótão reserva-se às áreas comuns; os quartos relegam-se a cave. O alpendre exterior confere-lhe um aspecto leviano e transpirável. Dentro, o pardo da nogueira do chão ressalta o reboco das paredes e o tom azeitonado da carpintaria.

I byggnaden, som är underordnad landskapet, kastas den konventionella distributionen om. Vindens transparens är reserverad för gemensamma utrymmen och sovrummen är förpassade till källaren. Användningen av lärkträ utomhus ger den ett lätt och luftigt utseende. Inomhus framhävs väggarnas puts och snickeriernas gröngula toner av det valnötsbruna golvet.

Ground floor

Second floor

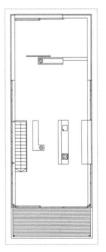

Third floor

BARN HOUSE

BURO II & ARCHI+I
Roeselare, Belgium
© Kris Vandamme

In order to give a residential feel to an old disused barn, the neat and careful intervention reincorporates the building into the surrounding landscape. As a greenhouse, a wooden laminate structure protects it from inclement weather and prying eyes. The interior decoration is the work of the artist Wim Delvoye.

Afin d'apporter une dimension résidentielle à une vieille grange abandonnée, l'intervention a consisté en une réintégration, prudente et minutieuse, du bâtiment dans le paysage alentour. Une structure laminaire en bois le protège des intempéries et du regard extérieur. La décoration intérieure est l'œuvre de l'artiste Wim Delvoye.

Mit dem Ziel, eine alte, ungenutzte Scheune in ein Wohnhaus umzuwandeln, hat der sorgfältige und behutsame Umbau das Gebäude auch wieder in die umgebende Landschaft aufgenommen. Wie eine Art Sonnendach schützt die Holzlamellenstruktur das Haus vor den Unbilden der Witterung und fremden Blicken. Die Innenausstattung ist ein Werk des Künstlers Wim Delvoye.

Met de bedoeling om de oude, in onbruik geraakte graanschuur bewoonbaar te maken, is gekozen voor een elegante en bedachtzame aanpak, waardoor het gebouw in het omringende landschap wordt opgenomen. Een plaatvormige, houten structuur doet dienst als afdak om schaduw te geven en om bescherming te bieden tegen weersomstandigheden en inkijk. De interieurinrichting is het werk van de kunstenaar Wim Delvoye.

Con el propósito de imprimir una dimensión residencial a un viejo granero en desuso, la intervención, pulcra y cautelosa, reincorpora el edificio en el paisaje que lo rodea. A modo de umbráculo, una estructura laminar de madera lo previene de las inclemencias del tiempo y las miradas ajenas. La decoración interior es obra del artista Wim Delvoye.

Con l'intento di trasmettere una dimensione residenziale a un vecchio granaio inutilizzato, l'intervento – attento e delicato – reinserisce l'edificio nel paesaggio circostante. Sotto forma di un pergolato, una struttura laminare in legno lo preserva dalle intemperie e dagli sguardi esterni. Gli arredi interni sono opera dell'artista Wim Delvoye.

Com o propósito de transmitir uma dimensão residencial a um velho celeiro em desuso, a intervenção, pulcra e cautelosa, reincorpora o edifício na paisagem que o rodeia. Como um umbráculo, uma estrutura laminar de madeira protege-o das inclemências do tempo e dos olhares alheios. A decoração interior é obra do artista Wim Delvoye.

I syfte att skänka en bostadsdimension åt ett gammalt nedlagt sädesmagasin återförenar ingreppet, ett prydligt och varsamt sådant, byggnaden med det omgivande landskapet. Som ett solskyddstak skyddar en laminatstruktur i trä mot dåligt väder och nyfikna ögon. Inredningen är ett verk av konstnären Wim Delvoye.

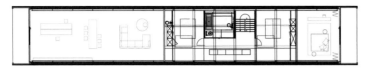

Second floor

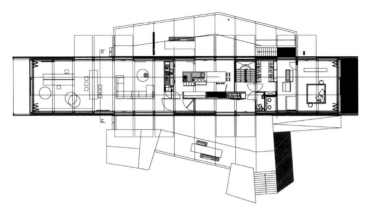

Ground floor

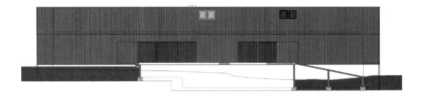

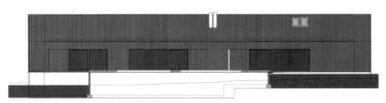

Building elevations

PRIVATE HOUSE IN **JŪRMALA**

ARHIS
Jūrmala, Latvia
© Ansis Starks

The original shape of the centenary house with its narrow windows is preserved, only its striking glazed veranda and its simple ash-gray wood cladding, like the tar colored fishing boats that anchored here in their day, distinguishe it from neighbouring buildings, with their attractive atavistics and adorned gables.

Cette maison centenaire conserve sa forme originale, dotée d'étroites fenêtres. Seul le caractère voyant de sa véranda en verre, associé à la sobriété de son revêtement en bois – cendré, comme le brai recouvrant les canots de pêches qui mouillaient jadis ici –, la distingue des autres constructions alentour, avec d'anciennes tourelles et des pignons ornés.

Dadurch, dass die Form des ursprünglichen, hundertjährigen Hauses mit seinen schmalen Fenstern erhalten blieb, unterscheidet es sich nur durch seine auffällige, glasverkleidete Veranda und seine nüchterne Holzbedachung – aschgrau, wie der Teer, der die seinerzeit hier liegenden Angelboote färbte – von den Nachbargebäuden mit ihren atavistischen Türmchen und verzierten Giebeln.

De vorm van het originele eeuwenoude huis met zijn smalle ramen is behouden en alleen de opvallende beglaasde veranda en de sobere houten bekleding –askleurig, net als de teer op de vissersboten die hier weleer voor anker gingen– maken dat het opvalt tussen de aangrenzende gebouwen met hun atavistisch torentjes en decoratieve puntgevels.

Conservando la forma de la casa centenaria original, con sus estrechas ventanas, sólo su llamativa veranda acristalada y su sobrio recubrimiento de madera –cenicienta, como la brea que teñía los botes pesqueros que en tiempos fondearan aquí– la distinguen de sus construcciones vecinas, con sus atávicas torrecillas y gabletes ornamentados.

Preservando la forma della struttura centenaria originaria con le sue strette finestre, solo la particolare veranda a vetrate e il sobrio rivestimento in legno – color cenere, come il catrame applicato sui pescherecci che un tempo attraccavano qui – la distinguono dagli edifici adiacenti, con le antiche torrette e i frontoni ornamentali.

Conservando a forma da casa original centenária, com as suas estreitas janelas, apenas a sua chamativa varanda envidraçada e o seu sóbrio revestimento de madeira - cinzenta, como o breu que tinham os botes pesqueiros que em tempos ancoraram aqui - a distinguem das suas construções vizinhas, com as suas atávicas torres e gabletes ornamentados.

Det är bara den slående glasverandan och den nyktra träbeläggningen – askgrå, som tjäran som färgade fiskebåtarna som förr låg förtöjda här – som särskiljer huset från de angränsande byggnaderna med sina atavistiska torn och smyckade gavlar. Detta eftersom man bevarat det ursprungliga hundraåriga husets form med sina smala fönster.

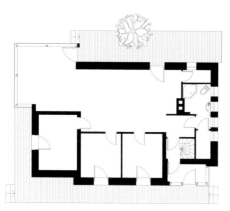

Floor plan

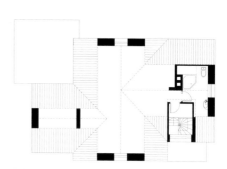

Roof

HOUSE IN **COLINA**

Felipe del Río, Federico Campino/OPA
Colina, Chile
© Nico Saieh, Cristina Alemparte

The house adopts the versatility of an agrarian structure: modular construction and large and expandable flexible spaces. A row of varying columns sustains the thermally insulated north roof and wall. Inside, a technical corridor, separated from the bedrooms by a brick wall, acts as a vestibule and meeting area.

La maison adopte le caractère versatile d'une structure agricole : une construction modulable et des espaces flexibles, vastes et extensibles. Une rangée de piliers de section variable soutient le toit et le mur nord, dotés d'une isolation thermique. À l'intérieur, un couloir technique – séparé des chambres par un mur en briques – sert à la fois de vestibule et de zone de réunion.

Das Haus übernimmt die Vielseitigkeit einer landwirtschaftlichen Struktur: Modularer Bau und flexible, großzügige und erweiterbare Bereiche. Eine Säulenreihe unterschiedlichen Durchmessers trägt das Dach und die Nordwand, die wärmeisoliert sind. Innerhalb dient ein technischer Flur – der von den Schlafzimmern durch eine Backsteinmauer getrennt ist, als Verteiler und Versammlungsraum.

Het huis neemt de veelzijdigheid van een agrarische structuur aan: een modulaire bouw en flexibele, ruime en vergrootbare ruimtes. Een rij pilaren met variabele doorsneden ondersteunt het dak en de muur aan de warmte-geïsoleerde noordzijde. Binnen doet een technische gang, van de slaapkamers afgescheiden door een bakstenen muur, dienst als ruimte om samen te zijn.

La casa adopta la versatilidad de una estructura agraria: construcción modular y espacios flexibles, amplios y ampliables. Una hilera de pilares de sección variable sujeta el techo y la pared norte, aislados térmicamente. Dentro, un pasillo técnico, separado de los dormitorios por un muro de ladrillo, actúa como distribuidor y área de reunión.

La casa adotta la versatilità di una struttura agraria: impianto modulare e spazi flessibili, ampi e ampliabili. Una fila di pilastri di sezione variabile sostiene il tetto e la parete nord, termicamente isolati. All'interno, un corridoio tecnico, separato dalle camere tramite un muro di mattoni, funge da disimpegno e area sociale.

A casa adopta a versatilidade de uma estrutura agrária: construção modular e espaços flexíveis, amplos e ampliáveis. Uma fileira de pilares de secção variável segura o tecto e a parede norte, termicamente isolados. Dentro, um corredor técnico, separado dos quartos por um muro de tijolo, actua como distribuidor e área de reunião.

Huset visar upp mångsidigheten hos en jordbruksstruktur, med sin modulära konstruktion och flexibla utrymmen, rymliga och utbyggbara. En rad pelare av variabel sektion bär taket och norra väggen som är värmeisolerade. Inomhus finns en teknisk korridor, avskild från sovrummen med en tegelvägg, som fungerar som genomgång och mötesrum.

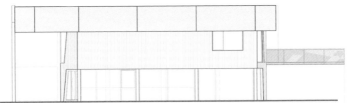

Building main elevation

Building side elevation

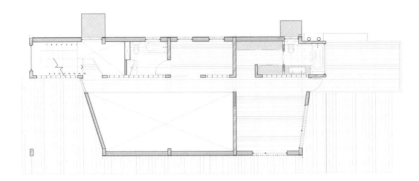

Second floor

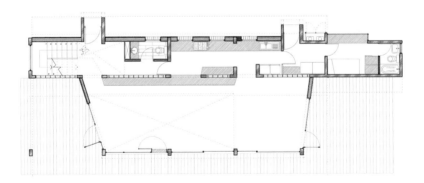

Ground floor

SHINGLE HOUSE

NORD Architecture
Dungeness, United Kingdom
© Charles Hosea, Living Architecture

The building seeks to compromise between the rigor of the climate and the aridity of the surrounding limestone desert. A layer of waterproof wooden panels with tar protects its prefabricated structure, matching the characteristic blackness of the local fishermen houses. Like a shining beacon, its chimney hints at the underlying polished concrete core.

L'édifice tend à s'adapter à la fois à la rigueur du climat et à l'aridité du désert calcaire qui l'entoure. Un revêtement en plaques de bois imperméabilisé à base de brai protège sa structure préfabriquée, lui conférant la noirceur typique des maisons de pêcheurs de la région. Tel un phare lumineux, sa cheminée fait ressortir le noyau en béton poli sous-jacent.

Das Gebäude versucht sich an die Strenge des Klimas und an die Trockenheit der Kalkwüste, die es umgibt, anzupassen. Eine Verkleidung aus mit Teer verdichteten Holzplatten schützt seine Fertighausstruktur, indem sie sie mit der typischen Schwärze der Fischerhäuser am Ort versehen. Wie ein glänzender Leuchtturm weist sein Kamin auf den darunterliegenden polierten Zementkern hin.

Het gebouw biedt een onderkomen in het strenge klimaat en de droogte van de omringende woestijn. Een laag van houten platen, waterdicht gemaakt met teer, beschermt de voorgefabriceerde structuur en geeft het de kenmerkende zwartheid van de plaatselijke vissershuizen. De schoorsteen suggereert, als een fonkelende vuurtoren, de kern van onderliggend gepolijst cement.

El edificio busca acomodo entre el rigor del clima y la aridez del desierto calizo que lo envuelve. Un manto de placas de madera impermeabilizada con brea protege su estructura prefabricada, ataviándola con la negrura típica de las casas de pescadores del lugar. Como un faro rutilante, su chimenea insinúa el núcleo de cemento pulido subyacente.

L'edificio si inserisce tra il rigore del clima e l'aridità del deserto calcareo che lo circonda. Un mantello di lastre di legno impermeabilizzato con catrame protegge la struttura prefabbricata, conferendole il colore scuro tipico delle case di pescatori della zona. Come un faro rutilante, il camino si inserisce nel nucleo di cemento lucido sottostante.

O edifício procura lugar entre o rigor do clima e a aridez do deserto calcário que o envolve. Uma capa de placas de madeira impermeabilizada com breu protege a sua estrutura pré-fabricada, adornando-a com a negrura típica das casas de pescadores do local. Como um farol rutilante, a sua chaminé destaca o núcleo de cimento polido subjacente.

Byggnaden strävar efter att passa in i det tuffa klimatet och den omgivande, karga kalkstensöknen. Ett täcke av träplankor behandlade med tjära skyddar den prefabricerade stommen och smyckar den med det typiska svarta från traktens fiskarehus. Som en lysande ledstjärna antyder skorstenen en underliggande kärna av polerad betong.

East elevation

West elevation

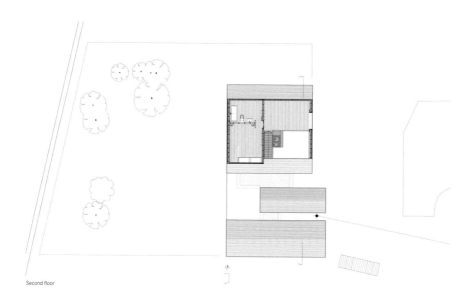

Second floor

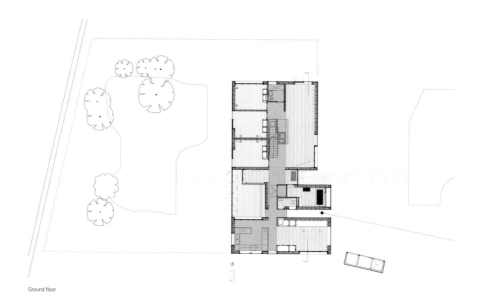

Ground floor

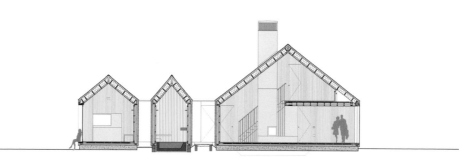

Building section

COUNTRY HOUSE IN **COLORADO**

Turnbull Griffin Haesloop Architects
Walden, CO, USA
© David Wakely Photography

In order to make the volume as compact as possible, the building is conceived as a Matryoshka of rectangles that are interconnected, fragmenting their spaces. Thus, the outer shell delimits the indoor area, which includes a covered area outside, and, inside, two white wooden blocks join the two halves of the second floor and flood the first floor with light.

Afin d'obtenir un volume compact, l'édifice a été conçu comme une série de poupées russes, avec des rectangles articulés entre eux, fragmentant ses différents espaces. Ainsi, le bloc externe délimite l'espace sous les toits, qui comporte une zone extérieure. À l'intérieur, deux cubes en bois blancs relient les deux moitiés du deuxième étage et permettent à la lumière de baigner le premier.

Um sein Volumen zu verdichten, ist das Gebäude wie eine Matroschka aus Rechtecken entworfen, die sich untereinander gliedern, indem sie ihre Bereiche aufspalten. Somit grenzt der äußere Kasten den überdachten Bereich ab, zu dem ein Außen- und ein Innenbereich gehören. Darin verbinden zwei Würfel aus weißem Holz die beiden Hälften der zweiten Etage und ermöglichen, dass das Licht die erste Etage ausfüllt.

Teneinde het volume compact te houden is het gebouw uitgedacht als een Matroesjka met rechthoeken die onderling verbonden zijn en de ruimtes verdelen. Op die manier bakent de externe doos de zone onder het dak af, waar zich tevens een overdekte buitenruimte bevindt. Van binnen worden de twee helften van de tweede verdieping verbonden door twee witte houten kubussen, waardoor er bovendien licht op de eerste verdieping komt.

A fin de compactar su volumen, el edificio se concibe como una *matriosca* de rectángulos que se articulan entre sí, fragmentando sus espacios. Así, la caja externa delimita el área bajo techo, que incluye una zona exterior a cubierto; dentro, dos cubos de madera blancos unen las dos mitades de la segunda planta y permiten que la luz bañe la primera.

Per compattarne il volume, l'edificio è pensato come una matrioska a rettangoli articolati tra loro, con una conseguente frammentazione degli spazi. Così la "scatola" interna delimita l'area del sottotetto che comprende una zona esterna al coperto; all'interno, due cubi di legno bianco uniscono le due metà del secondo piano e consentono alla luce di raggiungere il primo piano.

Com a finalidade de compactar o seu volume, o edifício concebe-se como uma Matrioska de rectângulos que se articulam entre si, fragmentando os seus espaços. Assim, a caixa externa delimita a área sob o tecto, que inclui uma zona exterior coberta; dentro, dois cubos de madeira brancos unem as duas metades do segundo piso e permitem que a luz banhe o primeiro.

För att komprimera volymen är byggnaden tänkt som en Matryoshka av sammanlänkade rektanglar, som delar upp utrymmena. På så vis avgränsar den yttre lådan utrymmet under tak där ett skyddat utomhusområde ryms, och inomhus med två vita träklossar som förenar andra våningens två halvor och tillåter ljuset att bada den första våningen.

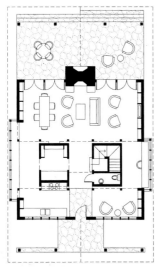

Ground floor

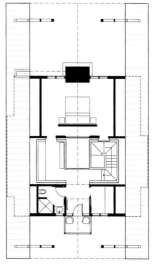

Second floor

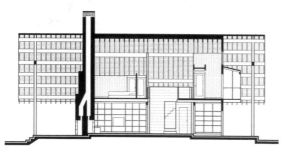

Building section – facing north

Building section – facing north

HOUSE IN **CERDEDILLA**

Pablo Fernández, Pablo Redondo
Madrid, Spain
© Arles Iglesias

Only the slate and granite were preserved from the old 1940s house. The interior was completely hollowed out, even the load-bearing walls. Instead, a huge bamboo unit containing the stairs, lets the light from the skylights flood the first floor, serves as storage space and connects the rooms.

De cette vieille bâtisse des années 1940, seule la structure en ardoise et granite a été préservée. L'intérieur a été entièrement vidé, y compris les murs porteurs. À la place, un immense meuble en bambou héberge les escaliers, laisse filtrer la lumière jusqu'au premier étage depuis les lucarnes du toit, sert d'espace de rangement et permet la communication entre les différentes pièces.

Von dem alten großen Haus aus den 40er Jahren blieb nur die Schale aus Schiefer und Granit erhalten. Der Innenraum - sogar die Stützmauern - wurde komplett geleert. An ihrer Stelle umfasst ein enormes Bambusmöbelstück die Treppe, lässt das Licht der Dachluken die erste Etage bestrahlen, dient als Lagerung und ermöglicht die Verbindung unter den Zimmern.

Van het grote oude huis uit de jaren 40 is alleen het leistenen en granieten frame overgebleven. Van binnen is het helemaal leeggehaald, inclusief de dragende muren. In plaats daarvan is er een enorm bamboe meubel dat de trap bevat, ervoor zorgt dat het licht dat door de dakramen valt de eerste verdieping bereikt, als bergruimte dient en verbinding tussen de kamers mogelijk maakt.

Del viejo caserón de los años cuarenta sólo se preservó su carcasa de pizarra y granito. El interior se vació por completo, incluso los muros de carga. En su lugar, un enorme mueble de bambú contiene la escalera, deja que la luz de los lucernarios del techo irradie el primer piso, sirve como almacenaje y permite la comunicación entre habitaciones.

Del vecchio casale degli anni '40 è stata preservata solo la struttura in lavagna e granito. L'interno è stato completamente svuotato, compresi i muri portanti. Al suo posto, un enorme mobile di bambù contiene la scala, fa sì che la luce dei lucernari del tetto illumini il primo piano, serve come contenitore e consente la comunicazione tra i vari ambienti.

Do velho casarão dos anos 40 apenas se preservou o seu exterior de xisto e granito. O interior esvaziou-se por completo, inclusive as paredes-mestras. No seu lugar, um enorme móvel de bambu que contém a escada, deixa que a luz das coberturas de vidro do tecto irradie o primeiro piso, serve como arrecadação e permite a comunicação entre divisões.

Från det gamla huset från 40-talet har endast höljet av skiffer och granit bevarats. Insidan tömdes helt, inklusive de bärande väggarna. Istället sattes ett enormt skåp av bambu in, vilket döljer trappan och släpper in ljuset från fönstren i taket till första våningen. Det fungerar både som förvaringsutrymme och som kommunikation mellan rummen.

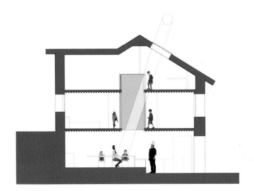

Section through kitchen

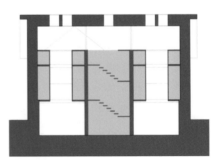

Longitudinal section

Built-in diagrams

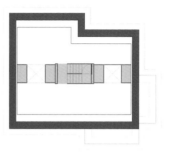

Attic

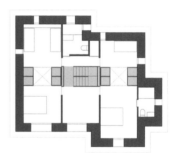

Second floor

Ground floor

HOUSE IN THE **PYRENEES**

Eduardo Cadaval, Clara Solà-Morales
Canejan, Spain
© Santiago Garcés

The building's original structure, imposed by its construction technique with thick, dense and opaque stone walls, converted it into an inverted bastion. After the intervention, the gabled roof, which does not rest on the walls, creates glass gallery pathways that flood the room with light and offer panoramic views of the Pyrenees.

La structure primitive de l'édifice, imposée par sa technique de construction – des murs en pierre épais, compacts et opaques – en faisait un bastion renfermé. Après réfection, le toit à deux pans, qui ne repose pas sur les murs, crée de chaque côté des galeries en verre qui baignent la pièce de lumière et offrent des vues presque panoramiques sur les Pyrénées.

Die ursprüngliche Struktur des Gebäudes, die durch seine Bautechnik aus dicken, kompakten und düsteren Steinmauern bedingt ist, hat es zu einer zurückgezogenen Bastion gemacht. Nach dem Umbau sind durch das Satteldach, das nicht auf den Mauern ruht, die beiden verglasten Galerien entstanden, die den Raum mit Licht füllen und panoramaähnliche Aussichten auf die Pyrenäen bieten.

De primitieve structuur van het gebouw, opgelegd door de bouwtechniek –dikke, compacte en ondoorzichtige, stenen muren–, maakte er een teruggetrokken bastion van. Na de verbouwing creëert het zadeldak, dat niet op de muren rust, even zo vele beglaasde galerieën die het vertrek in het licht zetten en bijna panoramische uitzichten over de Pyreneeën bieden.

La estructura primitiva del edificio, impuesta por su técnica constructiva –gruesos, compactos y opacos muros de piedra–, hizo de él un bastión retraído. Tras la intervención, el techo a dos planos, que no descansa sobre los muros, crea sendas galerías acristaladas que inundan la estancia de luz y ofrecen vistas casi panorámicas sobre los Pirineos.

La struttura iniziale dell'edificio, imposta dalla tecnica costruttiva impiegata - spessi, compatti e opachi muri di pietra - ne aveva fatto un bastione isolato. Dopo l'intervento, il tetto a doppio spiovente, che non poggia sulle pareti, crea numerose gallerie a vetrate che inondano l'ambiente di luce e offrono una vista quasi panoramica sui Pirenei.

A estrutura primitiva do edifício, imposta pela sua técnica construtiva - grossos, compactos e opacos muros de pedra –, fez dele um bastião retraído. Após a intervenção, o tecto de duas águas, que não descansa sobre os muros, cria caminhos envidraçados que inundam a estância de luz e cria uma vista quase panorâmica sobre os Pirenéus.

Byggnadens primitiva struktur, som följer av dess konstruktionsteknik med tjocka, kompakta och ogenomskinliga stenväggar, gjorde den till ett avskilt fäste. Efter ingreppet skapas gångar av glasgallerier som fyller rummet med ljus och ger nästan panoramautsikt över Pyrenéerna. Detta med hjälp av det gavelförsedda taket som inte vilar på väggarna.

Building elevations

Cross sections

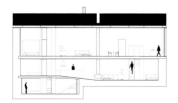

Longitudinal sections

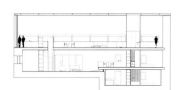

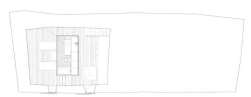

Ground floor

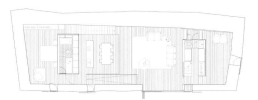

Second floor

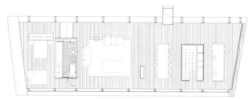

Third floor

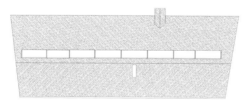

Roof

AHRENDSEE
HOUSE BY A LAKE

Pfeiffer Architekten
Saxony- Anhalt, Germany
© Jens Rötzsch

A plywood rib supports the single storey building and segments its interior. Its sloping roof is joined with its neighbor - a traditional German-Nowegian house - and its cladding, a layer of cedar boards, integrates it with the environment. Facing south, in front of the lake, a glass wall compensates for the narrowness of the rear windows.

Une nervure en contreplaqué soutient ce bâtiment à étage unique et segmente son intérieur. Sa toiture inclinée la relie à son voisin - une maison traditionnelle d'Allemagne du Nord - et son revêtement, un manteau en plaques de cèdre, lui permet de se fondre dans l'environnement. Orienté vers le sud, face au lac, un mur de verre compense l'étroitesse des fenêtres arrière.

Ein Rippengerüst aus Furnier trägt das Gebäude mit nur einer Etage und teilt seinen Innenraum auf. Das Schiefdach verbindet es mit dem Nachbardach, einem traditionellen norddeutschen Haus und seine Verkleidung aus Zedernplatten lässt es mit seiner Umgebung verschmelzen. Eine nach Süden, zum See ausgerichtete Glaswand gleicht die Schmalheit der Hinterfenster aus.

Een rib van gelaagd hout draagt het gebouw met alleen een benedenverdieping en segmenteert het interieur. Door het schuine dak is het verwant aan de naburige woning -een traditioneel Noord-Germaans huis- en de bekleding, een laag van cederhouten platen, doet het versmelten met de omgeving. Een glazen wand, georiënteerd naar het zuiden, aan het meer, compenseert de smalle ramen aan de achterzijde.

Una nervadura de contrachapado sostiene al edificio de planta única y segmenta su interior. Su inclinada cubierta la hermana con su vecino -una tradicional casa norgermánica-, y su revestimiento, un manto de placas de cedro, la funde con el entorno. Orientada al sur, frente al lago, una pared de cristal compensa la estrechez de las ventanas traseras..

Una nervatura di compensato sostiene l'edificio distribuito su un unico piano e ne segmenta l'ambiente interno. La copertura inclinata la rende simile all'edificio vicino - una casa tipica del nord della Germania - mentre il rivestimento, costituito da lastre di cedro, la integra nell'ambiente circostante. Orientata a sud, davanti al lago, una parete di vetro compensa le scarse dimensioni delle finestre posteriori.

Uma nervura de contraplacado suporta o edifício de um andar e segmenta o seu interior. O seu telhado inclinado como o da casa vizinha - uma casa tradicional alemã-norueguesa - e com o seu revestimento, uma camada de madeira de cedro, mistura-se com o ambiente. Virada para sul, em frente ao lago, uma parede de vidro compensa a estreiteza das janelas traseiras.

Korsande valvribbor i plywood bär upp denna byggnad som består av ett enda våningsplan och fungerar som avdelare för rummen inomhus. Det sluttande taket förenar huset med det angränsande traditionella nordgermanska huset, och fodringen av cederträ gör att det smälter in i miljön. En glasvägg mot söder, som vetter mot sjön, kompenserar för de smalare, bakre fönstren.

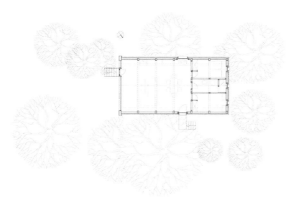

Floor plan

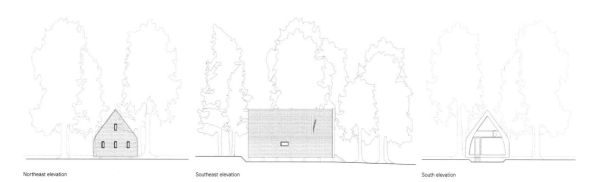

Northeast elevation

Southeast elevation

South elevation

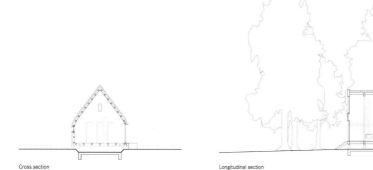

Cross section

Longitudinal section

AMSTERDAM LOFT

UXUS
Amsterdam, The Netherlands
© Dim Balsem

The original plan of a loft located in a former 18th century sugar warehouse has not been altered, barely changed in 250 years. A series of curtain-walls divides the space without compartmentalizing it. Made with Italian linen, the front of the curtains is totally opaque although totally translucent when viewed from behind.

Loft situé dans un ancien entrepôt de sucre du XVIIIᵉ siècle. Sans altérer le plan d'origine – à peine modifié en 250 ans – une série de murs-rideaux divisent l'espace sans le compartimenter. En lin italien, les rideaux sont opaques de face mais totalement translucides de dos.

Loft in einem alten Zuckerlager aus dem 18. Jahrhundert. Ohne den Originalplan – der in 250 Jahren kaum geändert wurde – zu verändern, trennt eine Reihe Wandvorhänge den Raum, ohne ihn einzuteilen. Die Vorhänge aus italienischem Leinen sind vorne blickdicht, aber von hinten komplett durchscheinend.

Loft gelegen in een voormalig suikerpakhuis uit de 18de eeuw. Zonder het originele project, dat in 250 jaar nauwelijks veranderd is, te wijzigen wordt de ruimte ingedeeld door een serie gordijnmuren, zonder deze te compartimenteren. De met Italiaans linnen vervaardigde gordijnen zijn frontaal gezien ondoorzichtig, maar helemaal licht doorlatend als ze van de achterkant worden bekeken.

Loft situado en un antiguo almacén de azúcar del siglo XVIII. Sin alterar el plan original –apenas modificado en 250 años–, una serie de paredes-cortina divide el espacio sin compartimentarlo. Confeccionadas con lino italiano, las cortinas son frontalmente opacas, aunque totalmente translúcidas al ser observadas desde detrás.

Loft situato in un antico magazzino di zucchero del '700. Senza alterare il progetto originario – rimasto praticamente uguale nel corso di 250 anni – una serie di pareti-tende divide lo spazio senza scomporlo. Realizzate con lino italiano, le tende sono opache se osservate frontalmente e totalmente traslucide se osservate da dietro.

Loft situado num antigo armazém de açúcar do século XVIII. Sem alterar a planta original – que ao longo de 250 anos não foi modificado –, uma série de paredes-cortina divide o espaço sem compartimentá-lo. Costuradas com linho italiano, as cortinas são frontalmente opacas ainda que totalmente translúcidas ao serem observadas por trás.

Ett loft beläget i ett gammalt sockerlager från sjuttonhundratalet. Den ursprungliga ritningen har nästan inte alls modifierats under 250 år, och utan att ändra den delas utrymmena upp med hjälp av gardinväggar, men utan att dela av dem helt och fullt. Gardinerna som är tillverkade av italienskt linne är helt täckande framifrån men genomskinliga sett bakifrån.

WEST BASIN HOUSE

Signer Harris Architects
Santa Fe, NM, USA
© Kira Gittings

The aesthetics of this modern ranch, designed and implemented remotely, betrays its conceptual boldness. Eclectic and functional, local tradition is distilled in spaces - kitchen, dining room, living room and courtyard -, and materials - masonry walls and columns and wooden beams -, as a native shroud over a modern, environmentally friendly and sustainable volume.

Le style de ce ranch moderne - conçu et réalisé à distance - trahit son audace conceptuelle. Éclectique et fonctionnel, il laisse filtrer la tradition locale au travers de certains espaces - cuisine, salle à manger, pièce à vivre, cour et matériaux - murs en maçonnerie, colonnes et poutres en bois - tel un manteau originel sur un corps moderne, écologique et durable.

Das Aussehen dieser modernen Ranch, die aus der Ferne entworfen und ausgeführt wurde, verrät ihr konzeptuelles Wagnis. Eklektisch und funktional filtert sie die lokale Tradition der Räume - Küche, Esszimmer, Wohnzimmer, Innenhof -, wie auch des Baumaterials - Mauerwerkmauern, Säulen und Holzträger - wie einen nativen Schleier über einem modernen, ökologischen und nachhaltigen Körper.

De esthetiek van deze moderne ranch -op afstand ontworpen en uitgevoerd- verraadt het gedurfde concept. De plaatselijke traditie sijpelt eclectisch en functioneel door in de vertrekken-keuken, eetkamer, zitkamer en patio- en in de materialen -metselwerk in natuursteen en zuilen en houten balken-, als een inheemse laag over het moderne, ecologische en duurzame hoofdbestanddeel.

La estética de este moderno rancho -diseñado y ejecutado a distancia- traiciona su atrevimiento conceptual. Ecléctico y funcional, destila la tradición local en espacios -cocina, comedor, sala de estar y patio- y materiales -muros de mampostería y columnas y vigas de madera-, como un manto nativo sobre un cuerpo moderno, ecológico y sostenible.

L'estetica di questo moderno ranch, progettato e realizzato da remoto, tradisce lo slancio concettuale. Eclettico e funzionale, applica la tradizione locale agli spazi - cucina, tinello, salotto e cortile - e ai materiali - pareti in muratura, colonne e travi in legno - come un manto nativo su un corpo moderno, ecologico e sostenibile.

A beleza deste moderno rancho - desenhado e executado à distância - atraiçoa o seu atrevimento conceptual. Ecléctico e funcional, destila a tradição local em espaços - cozinha, sala de jantar, sala de estar e pátio - e materiais - muros de alvenaria e colunas e vigas de madeira -, como um manto nativo sobre um corpo moderno, ecológico e sustentável.

Estetiken hos denna moderna ranch, designad och uppförd på distans, förråder dess begreppsmässiga djärvhet. Den är eklektisk och funktionell och ger uttryck för lokala traditioner i rum och material: kök, matsal, vardagsrum och innergård, och murade väggar och kolumner och träbjälkar. Som en inhemsk mantel på en modern, ekologisk och hållbar kropp.

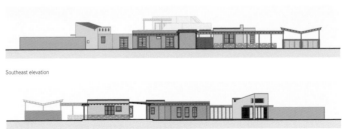

Southeast elevation

Northwest elevation

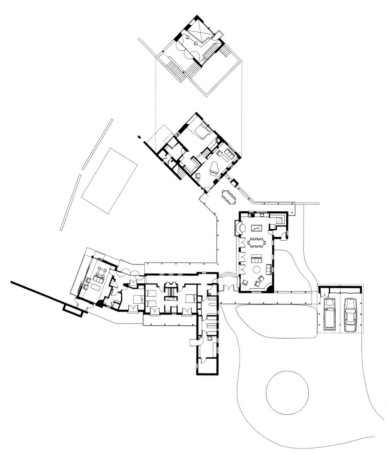

Site plan

Northeast elevation

Southwest elevation

CAN **SIMON**

Marià Castelló
Eïvissa, Spain
© EPDSE

This project updates this 19th-century estate without denaturing it, using the same construction techniques -wooden beams, stone masonry and lime cladding- and restored or reproduced materials of the original. Two new openings longitudinally cross the ground floor, creating a continuous and open-plan space.

Le projet remet au goût du jour cette exploitation agricole du XIXᵉ siècle, sans la dénaturaliser, en utilisant les techniques de construction – charpente en bois, maçonnerie en pierre et revêtement calcaire – et les matériaux – restaurés et reproduits – originaux. Deux nouvelles ouvertures traversent le rez-de-chaussée dans sa longueur, générant ainsi un espace continu et diaphane.

Das Projekt aktualisiert diesen Grundbesitz aus dem neunzehnten Jahrhundert ohne ihn zu denaturalisieren, indem es auf die gleichen Bautechniken zurückgreift: Holzbalken, Steinmauerwerk und Kalkverkleidung, sowie restaurierte Baumaterialien des Originals oder Nachbildungen. Zwei neue Öffnungen durchqueren das Erdgeschoss längs und bilden einen durchgehenden, leeren Raum.

Het project heeft deze negentiende-eeuwse herenboerderij gemoderniseerd zonder hem te vervormen, waarbij gebruik is gemaakt van dezelfde bouwtechnieken -houten balken, metselwerk in natuursteen en bekleding met kalk- en materialen -gerestaureerd of nagemaakt- dan het origineel. Twee nieuwe openingen zijn in de lengte door de benedenverdieping aangebracht, waardoor een continue en lichte ruimte verkregen wordt.

El proyecto actualiza esta hacienda decimonónica sin desnaturalizarla, recurriendo a las mismas técnicas constructivas -envigados de madera, mampostería de piedra y revestimiento de cal- y materiales -restaurados o reproducidos- del original. Dos nuevas aperturas atraviesan longitudinalmente la planta baja, generando un espacio continuo y diáfano.

Il progetto consiste nel riammodernare una struttura del XIX secolo senza snaturarla, ricorrendo alle stesse tecniche costruttive – travi di legno, pareti in pietra e rivestimento a calce – e materiali – restaurati o riprodotti – dell'originale. Due nuove aperture attraversano longitudinalmente il piano basso producendo uno spazio continuo e luminoso.

O projecto moderniza esta fazenda do século XIX sem desnaturalizá-la, recorrendo às mesmas técnicas construtivas – vigamentos de madeira, alvenaria de pedra e revestimento de cal – e materiais – restaurados ou reproduzidos – do original. Duas novas aberturas atravessam longitudinalmente o piso inferior, criando um espaço contínuo e diáfano.

I projektet aktualiseras denna hacienda från artonhundratalet utan att det blir onaturligt, med hjälp av samma byggnadsteknik och material som återfinns i den ursprungliga: träbjälkar, murverk av sten och kalkbeklädnad, restaurerade eller framställda material. Två nya, längsgående öppningar korsar nedre våningen och skapar ett kontinuerligt och ljust utrymme.

LA FINCA

UXUS
Mallorca, Spain
© Dim Balsem

The project provides a result in which the new is coupled to the old without dissonance. The restored interior of this 18th century white-washed house of rustic austerity contrasts with the sophistication of the furniture by Tom Dixon, Conran and Philippe Stark. In the garden, the pool appears to be suspended over an orange grove.

Le projet prévoit un ensemble mêlant le neuf et l'ancien dans une parfaite harmonie. L'intérieur restauré de cette ferme du XIIIᵉ siècle – sobre, blanc et rustique – contraste avec la sophistication des meubles signés Tom Dixon, Conran et Philippe Stark. Dans le jardin, la piscine s'élève au-dessus d'un verger d'orangers.

Das Projekt sieht einen Komplex vor, in dem sich das Neue stimmig an das Alte anpasst. Im restaurierten Innenbereich dieses Gehöfts aus dem 13. Jahrhundert hebt sich die rustikale weißtünchte Nüchternheit deutlich von der Geziertheit der Möbel von Tom Dixon, Conran und Philippe Stark ab. Im Garten scheint das Schwimmbad über einem Orangenobstgarten zu hängen.

Het project voorziet in een geheel waarin het nieuwe zich moeiteloos aan het oude verbindt. Het gerestaureerde interieur van deze hofstede uit de 13de eeuw, met een witgekalkte, landelijke soberheid, contrasteert met de geraffineerdheid van de meubels die ontworpen zijn door Tom Dixon, Conran en Philippe Stark. In de tuin lijkt het zwembad boven een sinaasappelboomgaard te hangen.

El proyecto prevé un conjunto en el que lo nuevo se acople a lo viejo sin disonancias. El restaurado interior de esta masía del siglo XIII, de blanqueada austeridad rústica, contrasta con la sofisticación de los muebles firmados por Tom Dixon, Conran y Philippe Stark. En el jardín, la piscina aparece suspendida sobre un huerto de naranjos.

Il progetto prevede la realizzazione di un complesso in cui nuovo e antico convivano in armonia. Il restauro precedente di questa residenza del 1200, dalla sbiancata austerità rustica, contrasta con la sofisticatezza dei mobili firmati da Tom Dixon, Conran e Philippe Stark. In giardino la piscina appare come sospesa su un aranceto.

O projecto prevê um conjunto no qual o novo se acople ao velho sem dissonâncias. O interior restaurado desta casa de campo do século XIII, de branqueada austeridade rústica, contrasta com a sofisticação dos móveis assinados por Tom Dixon, Conran e Philippe Stark. No jardim, a piscina aparece suspensa sobre um pomar de laranjeiras.

I projektet planeras en helhet där det nya passar ihop med det gamla utan dissonans. Restaureringen av interiören i denna katalanska bondgård från tolvhundratalet med vitkalkad, stram rustik, står i kontrast med de sofistikerade möblerna av Tom Dixon, Conran och Philippe Stark. I trädgården syns poolen som hängande över en apelsinlund.

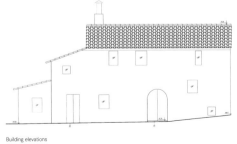

Building elevations

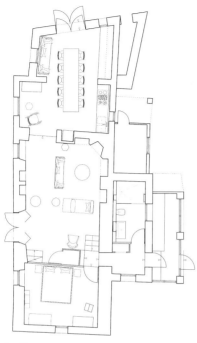

Ground floor

Second floor

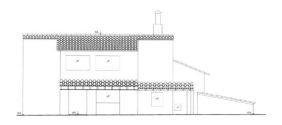

Building elevations

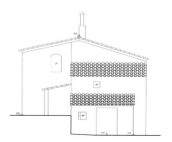

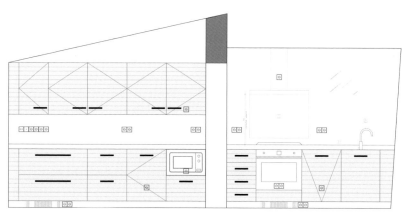

Kitchen elevation

MOUNTAIN RESEARCH

Shin Ohori, Setaro Aso/General Design
Kawakami-mura, Japan
© Daici Ano

With its entire native pine structure, the building – a creative shelter for a designer from Tokyo, is almost a kind of ephemeral architecture. Just a couple of gleaming The North Face® tents discusses the hegemony of the wood. Except for the bathroom, the living areas are relegated to external platforms positioned on different levels.

Avec sa structure intégrale en pin indigène, le bâtiment – un abri créatif appartenant à un designer tokyoïte – est presque une sorte d'architecture éphémère. Seules deux tentes de campagne The North Face® viennent rompre l'hégémonie du bois. À l'exception de la salle de bains, les espaces domestiques sont relégués sur des plateformes extérieures situées à différents niveaux.

Das Gebäude mit seiner kompletten Struktur aus bodenständiger Kiefer ist die kreative Zufluchtsstätte eines Tokioer Designers und fast ein Zufall kurzlebiger Architektur. Nur einige leuchtende The North Face® Zelte streiten dem Holz seine Hegemonie ab. Außer dem Bad sind die häuslichen Bereiche auf externe Plattformen verbannt, die sich auf unterschiedlichen Höhen befinden.

Met de geheel uit autochtoon grenenhout vervaardigde structuur is het gebouw – een creatief toevluchtsoord waarvan de eigenaar een uitwerper uit Tokio is – bijna een lotsbestemming van vluchtige architectuur. Alleen een aantal tenten van The North Face® bediscussiëren de hegemonie van het hout. Met uitzondering van de badkamer zijn de huiselijke vertrekken verschoven naar platformen buiten die op verschillende hoogtes liggen.

Con su estructura íntegra de pino autóctono, el edificio -un refugio creativo propiedad de un diseñador tokiota- es casi una suerte de arquitectura efímera. Sólo un par de rutilantes tiendas de campaña The North Face® discute la hegemonía de la madera. Salvo el baño, las áreas domésticas se relegan a plataformas exteriores situadas a distintos niveles.

Con una struttura interamente in pino locale, l'edificio – un rifugio creativo di proprietà di un designer di Tokyo – è quasi una sorta di architettura effimera. Solo un paio di fiammeggianti tende The North Face® si impongono contro l'egemonia del legno. Tranne il bagno, le aree domestiche sono relegate a piattaforme esterne distribuite su vari livelli.

Com a sua estrutura íntegra de pinho autóctone, o edifício – um refúgio criativo propriedade de um desenhador de Tóquio – é quase um tipo de arquitectura efémera. Apenas um par de rutilantes tendas de campanha The North Face® discute a hegemonia da madeira. Excepto a casa de banho, as áreas domésticas relegam-se para plataformas exteriores situadas a diferentes níveis.

Denna byggnad, med en struktur till fullo av inhemsk furu, är en kreativ fristad ägd av en Tokyodesigner, och utgör nästan ett slags efemär arkitektur. Bara några skimrande The North Face®-tält opponerar sig mot träets hegemoni. Med undantag för badrummet förpassas hushållsutrymmena till externa plattformar belägna på olika höjder.

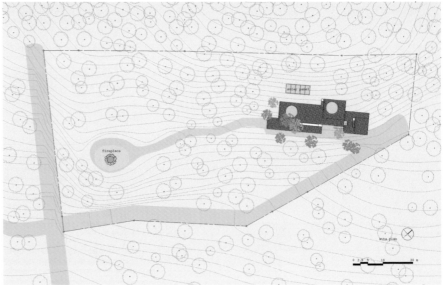

Site plan

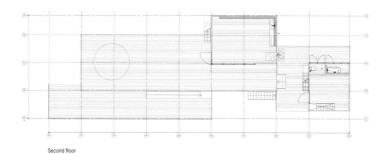

Second floor

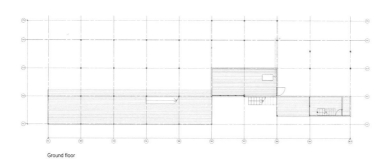

Ground floor

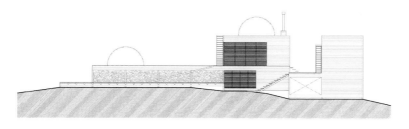

Building elevation

SHELL

ARTechnic Architects
Karuizawa, Japan
© Nacasa & Partners Inc.

This J-shaped shell consists of oval cylinders made from only two surfaces. Its smaller half protrudes sharply, sustaining the terrace at an altitude of 1,400 m above the sea. Adapted furniture has been used in the case where the structure would compromise the functionality of the space.

Cette carapace en forme de J comporte deux cylindres ovales composés à partir de deux surfaces uniques. Sa partie la plus petite ressort tout particulièrement, soutenant la terrasse à 1 400 mètres au-dessus du niveau de la mer. Là où la structure aurait pu compromettre la fonctionnalité de l'espace, on eut recours à des meubles adaptés.

Dieser Panzer in J-Form besteht aus zwei ovalen Zylindern, die ausgehend von nur zwei Oberflächen zusammengesetzt sind. Die kleine Hälfte ragt deutlich hervor und trägt auf 1.400 m Höhe über dem Meer eine Terrasse. Dort wo die Struktur die Funktionalität des Raumes beeinträchtigen könnte, hat man auf angepasste Möbel zurückgegriffen.

Dit J-vormige schild bestaat uit een aantal ovale cilinders die samengesteld zijn op basis van twee enige oppervlakken. De kleinste helft steekt geprononceerd uit en draagt het terras op 1400 m boven de zeespiegel. Daar waar de structuur de functionaliteit van de ruimte in gevaar zou kunnen brengen, heeft men naar aangepaste meubels gezocht.

Este caparazón en forma de J consta de un par de cilindros ovalados compuestos a partir de dos únicas superficies. Su mitad más pequeña sobresale pronunciadamente, sosteniendo la terraza a una cota de 1.400 m sobre el mar. Allí donde la estructura pudiera comprometer la funcionalidad del espacio se ha recurrido a muebles adaptados.

Questa corazza a forma di J comprende due cilindri ovali composti partendo da due uniche superfici. La metà più piccola sporge in modo deciso sostenendo la terrazza a 1400 m sopra il livello del mare. Nei punti in cui la struttura avrebbe potuto compromettere la funzionalità dello spazio, è stato fatto ricorso a mobili su misura.

Esta estrutura em forma de J consta de um par de cilindros ovais compostos a partir de duas únicas superfícies. A sua metade mais pequena sobressai pronunciadamente, sustendo o terraço a uma cota de 1400 m sobre o mar. Onde a estrutura pudesse comprometer a funcionalidade do espaço recorreu-se a móveis adaptados.

Detta J-formade hölje består av ett par ovala cylindrar som tillverkats utifrån endast två ytor. Den mindre halvan sticker ut på framträdande vis och bär upp en terass på 1400 meters höjd över havet. På de ställen där strukturen skulle kunna äventyra funktionaliteten i utrymmena har man använt anpassade möbler.

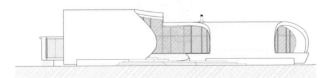

West elevation

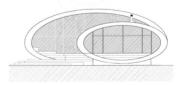

South elevation

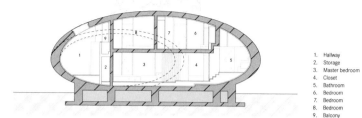

East/west section

1. Hallway
2. Storage
3. Master bedroom
4. Closet
5. Bathroom
6. Bedroom
7. Bedroom
8. Bedroom
9. Balcony

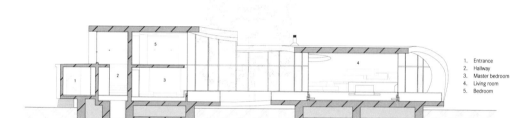

North/south section

1. Entrance
2. Hallway
3. Master bedroom
4. Living room
5. Bedroom

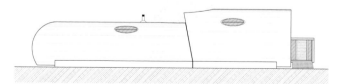

East elevation

North elevation

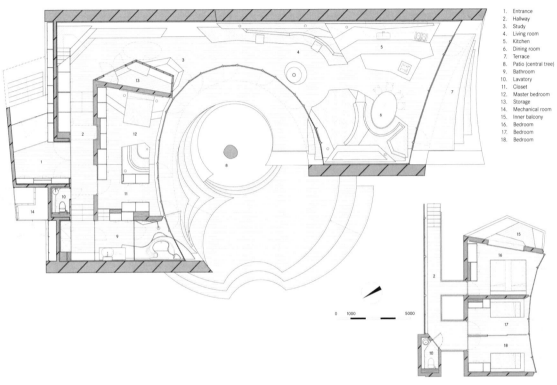

1. Entrance
2. Hallway
3. Study
4. Living room
5. Kitchen
6. Dining room
7. Terrace
8. Patio (central tree)
9. Bathroom
10. Lavatory
11. Closet
12. Master bedroom
13. Storage
14. Mechanical room
15. Inner balcony
16. Bedroom
17. Bedroom
18. Bedroom

0   1000   5000

Floor plan

VILLA **VALS**

Bjarne Mastenbroek/SeARCH, Christian Müller/CMA
Vals, Switzerland
© Iwan Baan

In order to circumvent the strict Swiss legislation in protected environments, a discrete and pragmatic intervention was chosen. By providing order to the complex around a spacious central patio, a slightly inclined façade was created offering beautiful views over the Alps. Under the adjacent stable, a tunnel accesses the house.

Afin de respecter la règlementation rigide de la Suisse en matière d'environnements protégés, les architectes ont opté pour une intervention discrète et pragmatique. L'agencement de l'ensemble autour d'une cour centrale donne naissance à une vaste façade légèrement inclinée qui offre des vues privilégiées sur les Alpes. Sous l'étable adjacente, un tunnel d'accès mène au logement.

Mit der Absicht, die strengen Schweizer Vorschriften in geschützten Umgebungen zu umgehen, entschied man sich für einen diskreten und pragmatischen Umbau. Indem der Komplex um einen zentralen Innenhof angeordnet ist, entsteht eine breite Fassade, die mit ihrer leichten Neigung bevorzugte Aussichten auf die Alpen bietet. Unter dem nebenliegenden Stall bietet ein Tunnel Zugang zum Haus.

Met de bedoeling om de strenge Zwitserse regelgeving in beschermde gebieden te omzeilen is gekozen voor een discrete en pragmatische aanpak. Bij het inrichten van het geheel rond een centrale binnenplaats is een brede gevel tot stand gekomen die, enigszins hellend, bevoorrechte uitzichten over de Alpen biedt. Onder de belendende stal biedt een tunnel toegang tot de woning.

Con la intención de sortear la rígida normativa suiza en entornos protegidos, se optó por una intervención discreta y pragmática. Al ordenar el conjunto alrededor de un patio central se genera una amplia fachada que, ligeramente inclinada, ofrece unas privilegiadas vistas sobre los Alpes. Bajo el establo adyacente, un túnel da acceso a la vivienda.

Nel rispetto della rigida normativa svizzera sulle aree protette, è stato scelto un intervento discreto e pragmatico. Distribuendo il complesso intorno a un cortile centrale nasce un'ampia facciata che, leggermente inclinata, offre un panorama privilegiato sulle Alpi. Sotto la stalla adiacente troviamo una galleria di accesso alla casa.

Com a intenção de contornar a rígida normativa suíça em ambientes protegidos, optou-se por uma intervenção discreta e pragmática. Ao ordenar o conjunto à volta de um pátio central gera-se uma ampla fachada que, ligeiramente inclinada, cria uma vista privilegiada sobre os Alpes. Sob o estábulo adjacente, um túnel dá acesso à moradia.

För att kringgå den stränga schweiziska lagstiftningen i skyddade miljöer valdes ett diskret och pragmatiskt ingrepp. Genom att ordna helheten kring en central innergård skapas en bred fasad som, aningens sluttande, lovar vackra vyer över Alperna. Under det angränsande stallet leder en tunnel till bostaden.

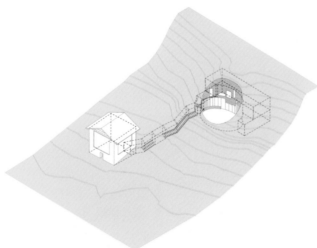

Connection diagram between new construction and existing barn

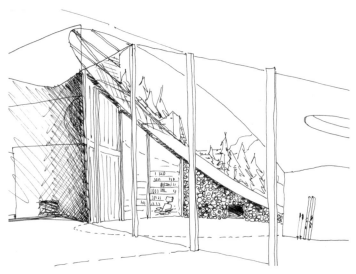

Preliminary sketch

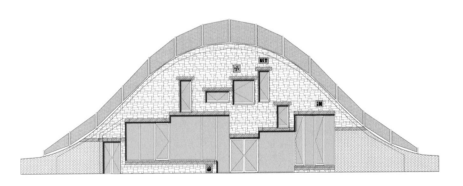

Front elevation

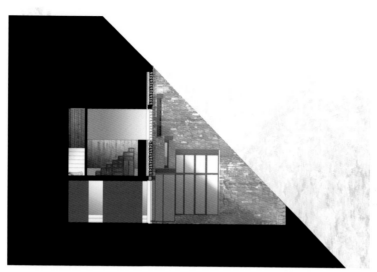

Building section

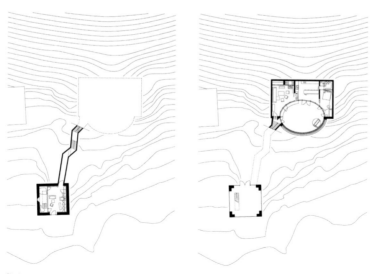

Site plans

Floor plans

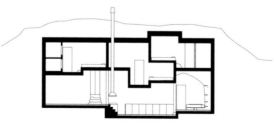

Section

ALEMANYS 5 HOUSE

Anna Noguera
Girona, Spain
© Enric Duch

Refurbishment of a Renaissance building that is trying to recover the pre-existing structure, altered by subsequent renovations, and adapt it to its new uses. The contrast between the materials used, cement and steel, stone and oak, and the abundant natural light give form to the volumes and shape and enhance the original features of the complex.

Rénovation d'un bâtiment de la Renaissance visant à récupérer la structure préexistante, altérée par diverses modifications successives, et à l'adapter à de nouvelles utilisations. Le contraste entre les matériaux utilisés – béton et acier, pierre et chêne – et l'abondance de lumière naturelle donnent forme aux volumes et font ressortir les caractéristiques originelles de l'ensemble.

Umbau eines Renaissancegebäudes, bei dem die bestehende, durch aufeinanderfolgende Änderungen veränderte Struktur an ihre neuen Zwecke angepasst werden soll. Der Kontrast zwischen den eingesetzten Baumaterialien – Zement und Stahl, Stein und Eiche – und der Fülle an Tageslicht verleihen den verschiedenen Volumina Form und heben die ursprünglichen Züge des Gesamten hervor.

Renovatie van een renaissancistisch gebouw, waarbij getracht is om de vooraf bestaande structuur, die door achtereenvolgende verbouwingen wijzigingen heeft ondergaan, te herstellen en aan te passen aan nieuwe gebruiken. Het contrast tussen de gebruikte materialen – cement en staal; steen en eikenhout – en het overvloedige hemellicht geven vorm aan het volume en versterken de originele kenmerken van het geheel.

Reforma de un edificio renacentista que trata de recuperar la estructura preexistente, alterada por sucesivas modificaciones, y adaptarla a sus nuevos usos. El contraste entre los materiales empleados –cemento y acero; piedra y roble– y la abundancia de luz natural dan forma a los volúmenes y realzan los rasgos originales del conjunto.

Ristrutturazione di un edificio rinascimentale che mira a recuperare la struttura preesistente, alterata da varie modifiche, adattandola al nuovo uso. Il contrasto tra i materiali utilizzati – cemento e acciaio, pietra e rovere – e l'abbondanza di luce naturale danno forma ai volumi ed evidenziano i tratti originali della struttura.

Remodelação de um edifício Renascentista que recupera a estrutura preexistente, alterada por modificações sucessivas, adaptando-o aos seus novos usos. O contraste entre os materiais utilizados, cimento e aço, pedra e carvalho, e a abundante natureza dão estrutura a volumes 3 e formas e melhoram as características originais do complexo.

En renoverad renässansbyggnad där man strävat efter att återställa den befintliga strukturen, vilken ändrats genom successiva modifieringar, och anpassa den till nya användningsområden. Kontrasten mellan cement och stål, sten och ek i materialanvändningen samt det rikliga naturliga ljuset formar kropparrna och framhäver de ursprungliga detaljerna i helheten.

Fourth floor. Apartment 2 – duplex

Second floor

1. Room
2. Room
3. Toilet
4. Lumber room
5. Hall
6. Installations
7. Garage
8. Stairs
9. Hall
10. Lounge/dining room
11. Bedroom
12. Bedroom
13. Bathroom
14. Patio
15. Garden
16. Stairs
17. Living room
18. Bedroom
19. Toilet
20. Bedroom
21. Toilet
22. Bedroom
23. Bathroom
24. Stairs
25. Lounge
26. Kitchen/dining room
27. Toilet
28. Veranda

Third floor. Apartment 2 – duplex

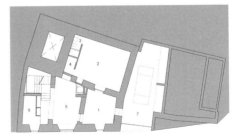

Ground floor

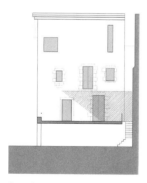

Cross section – garden

Cross section – lounge

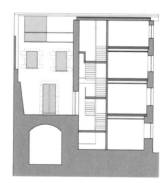

Cross section – patio

BARN REFURBISHMENT

Arteks Arquitectura
Arsèguel, Spain
© Eduard Comelles

Complete conversion of an old barn for residential uses. Outside, indigenous materials incorporate it into the surroundings: stone cladding, old Arabic tiles on the roof, and chestnut wood in the openings. Inside, it features open plan and frugal spaces: light wells, bare walls which are below the ceilings and floors without tiling.

Reconversion intégrale d'un ancien grenier à paille transformé en logement. À l'extérieur, des matériaux indigènes l'intègrent à son environnement : revêtement en pierre, tuile arabe vieillie sur la toiture et bois de châtaignier pour les ouvertures. À l'intérieur, des espaces diaphanes et épurés : des courettes, des murs nus qui n'atteignent pas le plafond et des sols non carrelés.

Vollständige Umwandlung einer alten Scheune für Wohnzwecke. Außen gleichen sie bodenständige Baumaterialien ihrer Umgebung an: Steinverkleidung, gealterte arabische Ziegel auf dem Dach und Kastanienholz an den Öffnungen. Drinnen leere und frugale Räume: Lichthöfe, nackte Wände, die nicht bis zur Decke reichen und ungekachelte Böden.

Volledige herstructurering van een oude strozolder om het voor bewoning geschikt te maken. Van buiten is gebruik gemaakt van inheemse materialen, waardoor de woning zich aan in de omgeving aanpast: stenen bekleding, verouderde holle dakpannen en kastanjehout in de openingen. Van binnen zijn er heldere en sobere ruimtes: lichtkokers, onbeklede muren die niet tot aan het plafond reiken en onbetegelde vloeren.

Reconversión integral de un viejo pajar para usos residenciales. Por fuera, materiales indígenas que lo asimilan a su entorno: revestimiento de piedra, teja árabe envejecida en la cubierta y madera de castaño en las oberturas. Dentro, espacios diáfanos y frugales: patios de luz, paredes desnudas que no alcanzan los techos y suelos sin embaldosar.

Riconversione integrale di un vecchio fienile per uso residenziale. Esternamente troviamo materiali autoctoni che fondono la struttura con il contesto circostante: rivestimento in pietra, tegole invecchiate sul tetto e legno di castagno sulle coperture. All'interno gli spazi sono luminosi e frugali: cortili di luce, parete nude che non raggiungono il soffitto e pavimenti senza piastrellatura..

Reconversão integral de um velho palheiro para usos residenciais. Por fora, materiais indígenas que o assemelham ao seu ambiente: revestimento de pedra, telha árabe envelhecida na cobertura e madeira de castanheiro nas aberturas. Dentro, espaços diáfanos e frugais: pátios de luz, paredes despidas que não alcançam os tectos e pavimentos sem lajes.

Fullständig omvandling av en gammal lada till bostad. På utsidan inhemska material som smälter in i omgivningen: stenbeklädnad, gamla arabiska tegelpannor på taket och kastanjeträ i öppningarna. Inomhus öppna och enkla ytor: innergårdar med ljus, nakna väggar som inte når taket och golv utan stenbeläggning.

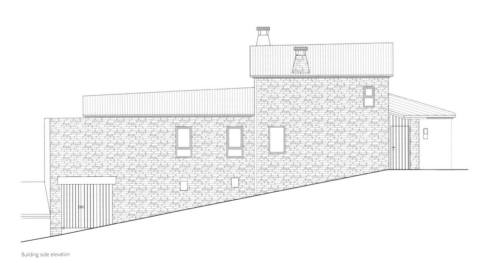

Building side elevation

1 m

1. Garage
2. Workshop
3. Hallway
4. Mechanical room
5. Bathroom
6. Multi-purpose room
7. Bedroom
8. Storage
9. Garden
10. Vegetable garden

Ground floor

1. Porch
2. Entry hall
3. Terrace
4. Kitchen/dining room
5. Living room
6. Hallway
7. Bedroom
8. Bathroom
9. Bedroom

Second floor

1. Bedroom
2. Bathroom

Third floor

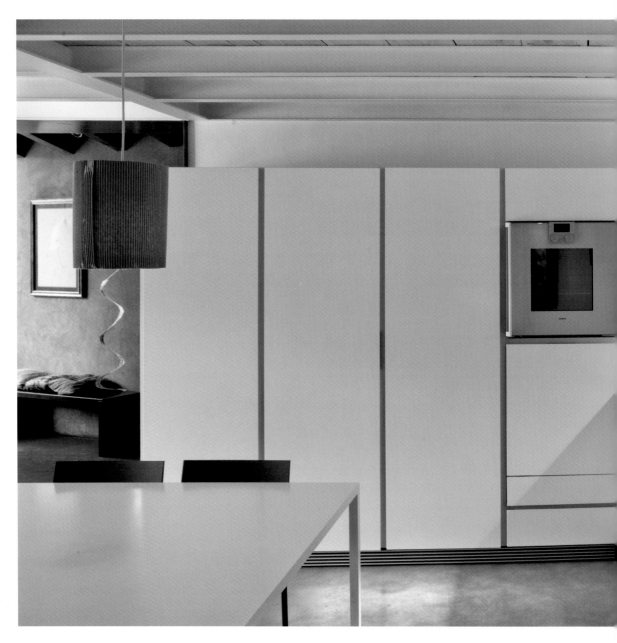

WEEKEND COTTAGE

Borja García, Sergio García-Gasco, Jorge Cortés
Alicante, Spain
© Borja García, Sergio García-Gasco

Small holiday home (25 m²/269 sq ft) designed as a compact block that respects local architecture and environment. The stonework of the façade is executed as retaining walls constructed from earth from the local area, populated mostly by a cherry orchard.

Cette petite résidence saisonnière – 25 m² de surface – est conçue en un bloc compact respectueux de l'architecture locale et de son environnement. La maçonnerie de la façade est à l'image des murs de contention des terres agricoles présentes dans la zone, en grande partie recouverte par un verger de cerisiers.

Kleines Ferienhaus mit nur 25 m² pro Etage, das als kompakter Block errichtet wurde und die lokale Architektur und Umgebung berücksichtigt. Das Mauerwerk der Fassade ist den Stützwänden der Agrarländereien dieser Region nachgebildet, die hauptsächlich mit Kirschgärten bepflanzt ist.

Kleine vakantiewoning met een grondoppervlak van 25 m² die ontworpen is als een compact blok waarin de plaatselijke architectuur en de omgeving gerespecteerd zijn. Het metselwerk in natuursteen van de gevel is uitgevoerd naar het voorbeeld van de keermuren van landbouwgrond die aanwezig zijn in de zone, die grotendeels in beslag wordt genomen door een kersenboomgaard.

Residencia vacacional de reducidas dimensiones –25 m² de planta– resuelta como un bloque compacto respetuoso con la arquitectura local y el entorno. La mampostería de la fachada está ejecutada a imagen de los muros de contención de tierras agrícolas presentes en la zona, poblada en su mayor parte por un huerto de cerezos.

Casa per le vacanze di piccole dimensioni – 25 m² – che si sviluppa come un blocco compatto che rispetta l'architettura locale e il contesto ambientale. La parte in muratura della facciata è realizzata riprendendo i muri di contenimento dei terreni agricoli della zona, caratterizzata principalmente dalla presenza di alberi di ciliegio.

Residência de férias de reduzidas dimensões – 25 m² de área – resulta como um bloco compacto que respeita a arquitectura local e o ambiente. A alvenaria da fachada está concebida à imagem dos muros de contenção de terras agrícolas presentes na zona, cultivada na sua maior parte por um pomar de cerejeiras.

Liten semesterbostad på 25 m² har lösts som ett kompakt block i överensstämmelse med den lokala arkitekturen och den omgivande miljön. Fasadens murverk är utformat som en avbild av de stödmurar som finns i områdets jordbruksmarker, som i huvudsak är bevuxna av en körsbärsträdgård.

215

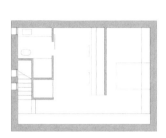

Basement

Ground floor

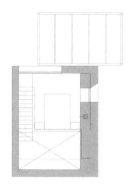

Second floor

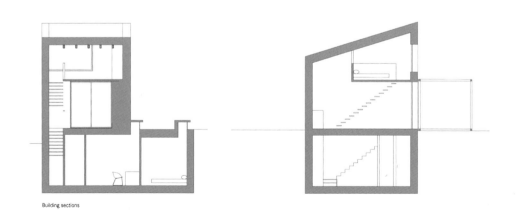

Building sections

East elevation

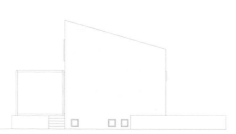

North elevation

West elevation

South elevation

HANSON HOUSE

David Salmela
Northeastern Minnesota, USA
© Peter Kerze

The house was carefully developed on bedrock, the vanishing point of its entire spatial distribution. Concrete pillars come out of the foundations that support the wooden structure. The terrace walls are inspired by the Muuratsalo house by Alvar Aalto, but in this case painted wooden slats replace the original brick.

La maison s'étend délicatement sur son lit rocheux, point de fuite de tout son agencement spatial. De ses fondations émergent des colonnes en béton qui soutiennent la structure en bois. Les murs de la terrasse s'inspirent de la maison Muuratsalo d'Alvar Aalto mais des baguettes en bois peint remplacent ici la brique d'origine.

Das Haus liegt sorgfältig auf einem Felsenbett angeordnet, welches den Fluchtpunkt der gesamten räumlichen Aufteilung darstellt. Aus seinem Fundament ragen Betonsäulen, die die Holzstruktur tragen. Die Wände der Terrasse sind am Muuratsalo Haus von Alvar Aalto inspiriert, aber in diesem Fall ersetzen lackierte Holzlatten den ursprünglichen Backstein.

De woning is zorgvuldig uitgespreid over de rotsachtige laag, het vluchtpunt van de hele ruimtelijke inrichting. Vanuit de fundering komen cementen pilaren naar boven, die de houten structuur ondersteunen. De muren van het terras zijn geïnspireerd op het huis Muuratsalo van Alvar Aalto, maar in dit geval worden de originele bakstenen vervangen door de latten van geverfd hout.

La casa se despliega cuidadosamente sobre el lecho rocoso, el punto de fuga de toda su distribución espacial. De sus cimientos emergen pilares de cemento que sustentan la estructura de madera. Las paredes de la terraza se inspiran en la casa Muuratsalo de Alvar Aalto, pero en este caso listones de madera pintada sustituyen al ladrillo original.

La casa si estende sul letto roccioso, punto di fuga dell'intera distribuzione spaziale. Dalle fondamenta emergono alcuni pilastri di cemento che sostengono la struttura in legno. Le pareti della terrazza ricordano la casa Muuratsalo di Alvar Aalto, ma in questo caso dei listoni di legno dipinto sostituiscono il mattone originale.

A casa desdobra-se cuidadosamente sobre o leito rochoso, o ponto de fuga de toda a sua distribuição espacial. Das suas fundações emergem pilares de cimento que sustentam a estrutura de madeira. As paredes do terraço inspiram-se na casa Muuratsalo de Alvar Aalto, mas neste caso tábuas de madeira pintada substituem o tijolo original.

Huset vecklar försiktigt ut sig på berggrunden, flyktpunkten för hela dess rumsliga fördelning. Från grunden reser sig betongpelare som bär upp stommen i trä. Terrassens väggar har inspirerats av Alvar Aaltos Muuratsalo-hus, men här har det ursprungliga teglet bytts ut mot målade träribbor.

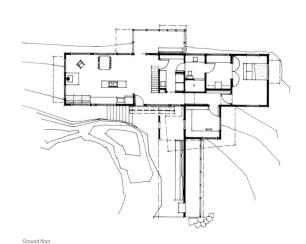

Ground floor

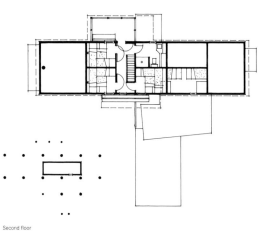

Second floor

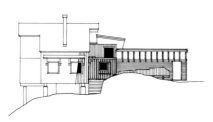

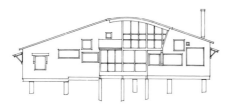

Building elevations

FLINT HOUSE

Nick Willson Architects
Blackheath, London, United Kingdom
© Gareth Gardner

This both functional and sustainable custom-made house combines new technology and craftsmanship. The result is a tapestry of nuanced textures where every detail has been taken into account. Something that is evident in the wooden beams or walls covered with flint, on the lead roofs or in the woodwork.

Cette maison faite sur mesure, aussi fonctionnelle que durable, conjugue nouvelle technologie et artisanat. Le résultat obtenu est une tapisserie de textures riche en nuances et dans laquelle chaque détail a été étudié avec soin. On peut notamment le constater sur la charpente en bois, sur les murs recouverts de silex, ou encore sur les toitures en plomb ou la charpenterie.

Bei diesem maßgeschneiderten - genauso funktionalen wie nachhaltigen - Haus, werden neue Technologie und Kunsthandwerk konjugiert. Das Ergebnis ist ein Gewebe aus reichhaltigen Texturen, bei dem jede Einzelheit sorgfältig gepflegt wurde. Das erkennt man an der Balkenstruktur aus Holz, den mit Feuerstein bedeckten Wänden, den Bleiabdeckungen oder an der Tischlerei.

Dit op maat gemaakte huis, dat zowel functioneel als duurzaam is, combineert nieuwe technologie met ambachtswerk. Het resultaat is een tapijt van texturen, rijk aan nuances, waarin over ieder detail zorgvuldig is nagedacht. Dit is te zien in de houten balken of in de met vuursteen beklede muren; in de loden daken of in de kozijnen.

Esta casa hecha a medida, tan funcional como sostenible, conjuga nueva tecnología y artesanía. El resultado es un tapiz de texturas rico en matices donde cada detalle se ha cuidado con esmero, algo apreciable en el envigado de madera o en las paredes recubiertas de pedernal, en las cubiertas de plomo o en la carpintería.

Questa casa realizzata su misura, funzionale e sostenibile allo stesso tempo, coniuga nuove tecnologie e fattura artigianale. Il risultato è un insieme di finiture ricco di sfumature, dove ogni dettaglio è curato nel dettaglio. Lo si apprezza nelle travi di legno o le pareti ricoperte di selce, nei rivestimenti di piombo o nelle parti in legno.

Esta casa personalizada, funcional e sustentável, conjuga nova tecnologia com artesanato. O resultado é uma tapeçaria de diferenciadas texturas onde todos os detalhes foram cuidadosamente trabalhados. Algo que se nota nas vigas de madeira ou paredes cobertas de sílex, nos telhados de chumbo ou carpintaria.

Detta hus byggdes efter beställning och är lika funktionellt som hållbart. Här kombineras ny teknik med hantverk. Resultatet är en väv av nyanserade texturer där alla detaljer har vårdats med omsorg. Det är aningen märkbart i träbjälkarna eller i väggarna täckta med flinta, i blytaken eller i snickerierna.

Preliminary sketch

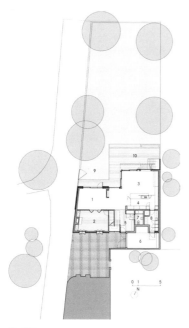

Ground floor

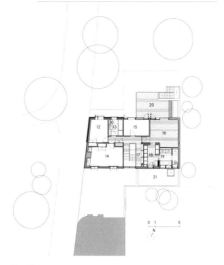

Second floor

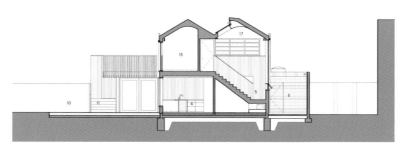

Building section

1. Living room
2. Snug
3. Dining room
4. Kitchen
5. Hall/entrance
6. Garage
7. Toilet
8. Utility room
9. Garage
10. Evening terrace
11. External stair
12. Bedroom
13. Family bathroom
14. Bedroom
15. Study
16. Master bedroom
17. Library
18. Dressing
19. Master bathroom
20. Evening terrace
21. Green roof

MARCUS BEACH HOUSE

Bark Design Architects
Noosa, Australia
© Cristopher Frederick Jones

The home is divided by two pavilions embracing a centenary ash. To the south, there is a permeable space irradiated by the light of the neighboring coast, and facing north, a room is attached to a garden that insulates it acoustically. A series of holes and corners create evocative lighting effects everywhere acting as hinges connecting the space.

La résidence s'articule au travers de deux pavillons autour d'un frêne centenaire. Au sud, un espace perméable est baigné de lumière provenant de la côte voisine ; face au nord, se trouve un abri adossé à un jardin qui lui procure une isolation sonore. De toutes parts, une multitude de trous et de recoins, semblables à des charnières reliant l'ensemble, génèrent des jeux de lumières surprenants.

Das Wohnhaus ist in zwei Pavillons gegliedert, die eine hundertjährige Esche umrahmen. Im Süden liegt ein durchlässiger, vom Licht der nahen Küste bestrahlter Bereich. Richtung Norden befindet sich ein Wohnraum, der an einen Garten als akustische Isolierung gelegt wurde. Überall bilden Öffnungen und Winkel – wie Scharniere, die ein Ganzes bilden – anregende Lichtspiele.

De woning is onderverdeeld in twee paviljoens die een honderd jaar oude es omarmen. Op het zuiden schijnt het licht van de dichtbij gelegen kust naar binnen; op het noorden dient een aan de tuin grenzend vertrek als geluidsisolatie. Overal genereren een serie openingen en hoeken, die als scharnieren die het geheel met elkaar verbinden, suggestieve lichtspelen.

La residencia se articula mediante dos pabellones que abrazan un fresno centenario. Al sur, un espacio permeable irradiado por la luz de la vecina costa; apuntando al norte, un habitáculo adosado a un jardín que lo aísla acústicamente. Por doquier, como goznes trabando el conjunto, una serie de huecos y rincones genera sugerentes juegos de luces.

L'abitazione si articola in due padiglioni che abbracciano un frassino centenario. A sud, uno spazio permeabile irradiato dalla luce della costa vicina; a nord, un piccolo ambiente addossato a un giardino che lo isola acusticamente. Ovunque, come tanti perni che perforano la struttura, una serie di buchi e angoli produce suggestivi giochi di luci.

A residência articula-se através de dois pavilhões que abraçam um freixo centenário. Ao sul, um espaço permeável irradiado pela luz da vizinha costa; orientado a norte, um habitáculo encostado a um jardim que o isola acusticamente. Por toda a parte, como dobradiças a trabalhar o conjunto, uma série de espaços e recantos cria sugestivos jogos de luzes.

Bostaden uppdelas med två paviljonger som omsluter en hundraårig ask. I söder ett utrymme där ljuset från den närbelägna kusten tränger in, i norr ett rum hopbyggt med en trädgård som fungerar ljudisolerande. Överallt, som gångjärn som förenar helheten, skapar ett antal hålrum och kanter suggestiva ljuseffekter.

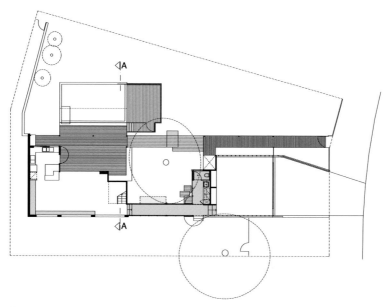

Floor plan

Building section and elevation

0   5

Building elevation

Building elevation

ERLANDSON VILLA

Per Friberg Arkitektbyrå
Ljunghusen, Sweden
© Åke E:Son Lindman

An orthogonal structure of posts and beams sustains the house, whose outer walls are supported by two posts. Wood is the predominant material inundating the shape and fusing it with the landscape. Its southern façade opens to a clearing that warms and nourishes it with light. The finishes, such as the eaves or joints, have been meticulously cared for to give the whole structure an imposing presence.

Une structure octogonale, composée de poteaux et de poutres, supporte la maison, dont les murs extérieurs reposent sur des montants. La prédominance du bois dissimule la forme de la construction qui se fond dans le paysage. Sa façade sud s'ouvre sur une clairière qui la baigne de lumière et de chaleur. Les finitions, comme les auvents et les jointures, ont été réalisées avec soin afin de donner de l'allure à l'ensemble.

Eine Rechteckstruktur aus Pfosten und Trägern trägt das Haus, dessen Außenwände auf zwei Diagonalstützen aufliegen. Das Holz herrscht soweit vor, dass es die Form erdrückt und sie mit der Landschaft verschmelzt. Die Südfassade öffnet sich zu einer Lichtung hin, von der sie Wärme und Licht erhält. Die Ausführungen wie Vordächer oder Verbindungen wurden sorgfältig gepflegt, um dem Komplex Eindruck zu verleihen.

Het huis wordt gedragen door een rechthoekige structuur van staanders en balken en de buitenmuren steunen op even zovele steunbalken. Hout heeft de overhand en laat de vorm met het landschap versmelten. De zuidgevel opent zich naar een lichtopening die zorgt voor warmte en licht. De afwerkingen, zoals overstekende dakranden en verbindingsstukken, zijn zorgvuldig uitgedacht, om het geheel voornaamheid te geven.

Una estructura ortogonal de postes y vigas sujeta la casa, cuyas paredes externas se apoyan en sendos montantes. La madera predomina hasta ahogar la forma y fundirla con el paisaje. Su fachada sur se abre a un claro que la caldea y la nutre de luz. Los acabados, como aleros o junturas, han sido minuciosamente cuidados para dar empaque al conjunto.

Una struttura ortogonale con piloni e travi sostiene la casa, le cui pareti esterne poggiano su vari montanti. Il legno predomina fino a soffocare la forma e fonderla con il paesaggio. La facciata sud si apre su una radura che la riscalda e la nutre di luce. Le finiture, come grondaie o giunzioni, sono curate nei minimi dettagli per dare enfasi al complesso.

Uma estrutura ortogonal de postes e vigas segura a casa, cujas paredes externas se apoiam em grandes pilares. A madeira predomina até afogar a forma e fundi-la com a paisagem. A sua fachada sul abre-se para uma clareira que a aquece e a nutre de luz. Os acabamentos, como telhados avançados e juntas, foram minuciosamente cuidados para dar impacto ao conjunto.

En ortogonal struktur med stolpar och bjälkar bär upp huset, vars ytterväggar stöds på varsin stödpelare. Här dominerar trä till den grad att formen kvävs och smälter in i landskapet. Söderväggen öppnar upp mot en glänta som tillhandahåller värme och ljus. Detaljer som takutsprång och fogar har vårdats in i minsta detalj för att ge det hela fin hållning.

Site plan

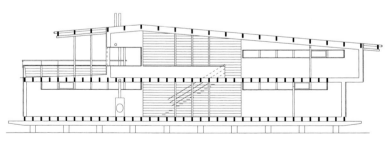

Building section

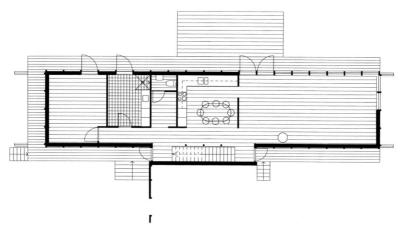

Second floor

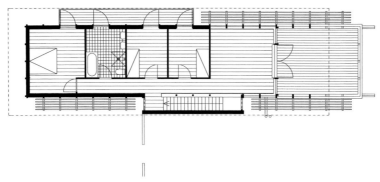

Ground floor

BALA PARK

Altius Architecture
Lake Muskoka, Canada
© Jonathan Savoie

The ground floor of the building, with varying ceiling heights depending on the terrain, lies on a bed of granite that, in turn, anchors the first floor to the Canadian Shield. At ground level, the exposed Douglas fir roof gives rhythm and consistency to the space. Above, the sloping roof reveals the granite through skylights.

Le rez-de-chaussée du bâtiment, avec des plafonds de hauteur variable en fonction du terrain, repose sur un massif de granite qui, à son tour, intègre le premier étage au paysage du bouclier canadien. Au ras du sol, le toit épuré en sapin de Douglas apporte du rythme et de la cohésion à l'espace. Au sommet, l'inclinaison du toit révèle le granite au travers des vitres.

Das Erdgeschoss des Gebäudes, mit unterschiedlich hohen Decken je nach Gelände, liegt auf einem Granitmassiv, welches wiederum die erste Etage am Kanadischen Schild verankert. Auf Bodenhöhe verleiht die freigelegte Decke aus Douglas-Tannenholz dem Raum Rhythmus und Kohäsion. Oben enthüllt die Dachneigung den Granit über Dachfenster.

De begane grond van de woning, met daken van verschillende hoogtes, afhankelijk van het terrein, staat op een granieten massief dat de eerste verdieping op het Canadese Schild verankert. Laag bij de grond, geeft het dak van Douglassparren de ruimte ritme en samenhang en boven onthult de helling van het dak het graniet via dakramen.

La planta baja del inmueble, con techos de altura variable en función del terreno, yace sobre un macizo de granito que, a su vez, ancla la primera planta al escudo Canádico. A ras de suelo, el techo de abeto de Douglas, descubierto, da ritmo y cohesión al espacio; arriba, la inclinación del tejado revela el granito a través de lucernarios.

Il piano terra dell'edificio, con soffitti di altezza variabile in base al terreno, poggia su un massiccio di granito che, a sua volta, ancora il primo piano allo scudo canadese. Al livello del terreno, il soffitto di abete di Douglas, scoperto, dà ritmo e coesione allo spazio; in alto, l'inclinazione del soffitto rivela il granito da alcuni lucernari.

O piso inferior do imóvel, com tectos de altura variável em função do terreno, assenta sobre um maciço de granito que, por sua vez, ancora o primeiro piso ao escudo canadiano. Ao nível do chão, o tecto de abeto de Douglas, descoberto, dá ritmo e coesão ao espaço; em cima, a inclinação do telhado revela o granito através de lucernários.

Byggnadens bottenvåning, med sin varierande takhöjd beroende på markhöjd, vilar på en bädd av granit som i sin tur förankrar första våningen till den kanadensiska skölden. På marknivå ger det öppna taket av douglasgranträ rytm och sammanhållning till utrymmet. Ovanför avslöjar takens lutning granit via takfönster.

MAURER HOUSE

Florian Maurer/Allen + Maurer Architects Ltd.
Toten, Norway
© Florian Maurer, Stuart Bish

Standing on the bedrock and without disturbing the existing vegetation, the house sits on the landscape without distorting it. Its configuration, four autonomous units around a garden, one towering above the landscape, ensures the privacy of its residents. The glulam structure that holds it, in turn, supports the windows.

Dressée sur son lit rocheux, sans aucune altération de la végétation préexistante, la maison prend racine dans le paysage sans le dénaturer. Sa configuration - quatre unités autonomes autour d'un jardin, l'une d'elles se détachant du paysage - assure l'intimité de ses résidents. La structure de lamellé-collé qui la soutient supporte également les verrières.

Über einem Felsbett und ohne die bestehende Landschaft zu verändern, ist das Haus derart in der Landschaft verwurzelt, dass es sie nicht verfälscht. Sein Gestaltung - aus vier eigenständigen Einheiten um einen Garten herum, von denen eine über die Landschaft hinausragt - gewährleistet die Privatsphäre seiner Bewohner. Die tragende Struktur von BSH trägt gleichzeitig die Fensterfronten.

Dit huis, dat zich boven de rotsachtige grond verheft zonder de voorbestaande begroeiing te wijzigen, schiet wortel in een landschap zonder het te ontkrachten. De configuratie - vier zelfstandige eenheden rond een tuin, waarvan een boven het landschap uitsteekt- garandeert de privacy van de bewoners. De structuur van gelamineerd hout waardoor hij ondersteund wordt, draagt tevens de ramen.

Erguido sobre el lecho rocoso y sin alterar la vegetación preexistente, la casa arraiga en el paisaje sin desvirtuarlo. Su configuración -cuatro unidades autónomas en torno a un jardín, una de ellas destacándose sobre el paisaje- garantiza la privacidad de sus residentes. La estructura de madera laminada pegada que la sujeta soporta a su vez las cristaleras.

Innalzata su un letto roccioso senza alterare la vegetazione preesistente, la casa è radicata nel paesaggio rispettandolo. La sua configurazione - quattro unità autonome che si sviluppano intorno a un giardino, una delle quali si innalza sul paesaggio circostante - garantisce la privacy di chi vi abita. La struttura in legno lamellare incollato che la sostiene supporta anche le vetrate.

Erguido sobre o leito rochoso e sem alterar a vegetação preexistente, a casa enraíza na paisagem sem desvirtuá-la. A sua configuração - quatro unidades autónomas em torno de um jardim, uma delas destacando-se sobre a paisagem - garante a privacidade dos seus residentes. A estrutura de madeira laminada colada que a suporta por sua vez as vidraças.

Huset är rest på berggrunden och utan att störa befintlig växtlighet är det förankrat i landskapet utan att förvränga det. Kompositionen av fyra självständiga enheter omkring en trädgård, varav en reser sig över landskapet, garanterar de boendes privatliv. Den bärkraftiga stommen av limträ uppbär i sin tur glaset.

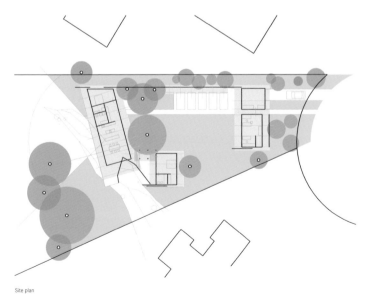

Site plan

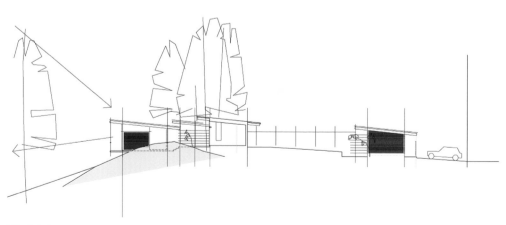

Building side elevation

LAKE WENATCHEE RESIDENCE

DeForest Architects
Washington, WA, USA
© Ben Benschneider

The house, with two different volumes, emerges from the landscape like a rock formation. The top half contains the bedrooms; the lower part contains the kitchen, the living room – with hidden access to the screening room behind a bookcase - and the porch. Their warm colors and textures complement those of the landscape.

La maison, composée de deux volumes séparés, émerge du paysage telle une formation rocheuse. La moitié supérieure comporte deux chambres tandis que, dans la partie inférieure, un pavillon vitré héberge la cuisine, la pièce à vivre - avec un accès caché à la salle de projection *via* une bibliothèque - ainsi que le porche. Ses couleurs et textures, dans les tons chauds, rappellent celles du paysage.

Das Haus mit zwei unterschiedlichen Volumina ragt wie eine Felsenformation aus der Landschaft hervor. Die obere Hälfte enthält die Schlafzimmer. In der unteren Hälfte umfasst ein verglaster Pavillon Küche, Wohnzimmer - mit Geheimzugang zum Vorführsaal hinter einer Bücherwand - und Vorhalle. Seine Farben und Texturen in warmen Tönen passen zu denen der umgebenden Landschaft.

Het huis, met twee verschillende volumes, doemt als een rotsformatie op uit het landschap. De bovenste helft omvat de slaapkamers, op de onderste helft bevinden zich, in een beglaasd paviljoen, de keuken, zitkamer - met verborgen toegang tot de filmzaal achter een boekenkast - en overdekte galerij. De kleuren en texturen, in warme tonen, komen terug in die van het landschap zelf.

La casa, con dos volúmenes diferenciados, emerge del paisaje como una formación rocosa. La mitad superior contiene los dormitorios; en la inferior, un pabellón acristalado guarda cocina, sala de estar -con acceso oculto a la sala de proyecciones tras una librería- y porche. Sus colores y texturas, de tonos cálidos, redundan en los del paisaje mismo.

La casa, con due volumi differenziati, emerge dal paesaggio come una formazione rocciosa. La metà superiore ospita le camere; in quella inferiore un padiglione a vetrate contiene cucina, salotto - con accesso nascosto alla sala proiezioni dietro una libreria - e il porticato. I colori e le finiture, dai toni caldi, richiamano quelli del paesaggio circostante.

A casa, com dois volumes diferenciados, emerge da paisagem como uma formação rochosa. A metade superior contém os quartos; na inferior um pavilhão envidraçado guarda cozinha, sala de estar - com acesso escondido à sala de projecções por trás de uma estante - e alpendre. As suas cores e texturas, de tons quentes, redundam nas mesmas da paisagem.

Huset med två olika kroppar dyker upp ur landskapet som en klippformation. Den övre halvan hyser två sovrum, den nedre en glaspaviljong där kök, vardagsrum och veranda ryms. Vardagsrummet med en dold ingång bakom en bokhylla till projektorrummet. Färger och texturer i varma toner gagnar landskapets samma sådana.

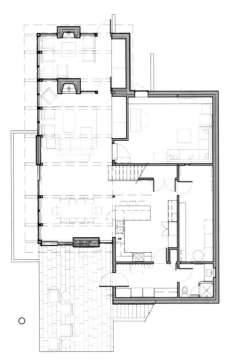

Ground floor

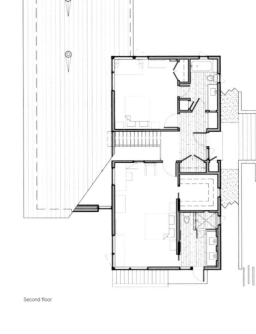

Second floor

HOUSE ON **MOUNT FUJI**

Satoshi Okada
Narusawa Village, Japan
© Hiroyuki Hirai

The building looks like a solidified lava sculpture, with its black-stained cedar coating, sheltered by a lush forest. A wall diagonally crosses the house and divides the living areas from the bedrooms. From the entrance, a narrow corridor widens to lead to a gallery in which a narrow skylight roof shines.

L'édifice, en raison de son revêtement en cèdre teinté en noir ressemble à une sculpture en lave solidifiée, abritée par une forêt abondante. Une cloison traverse l'ensemble dans sa diagonale et sépare la zone commune des pièces à vivre. Depuis l'entrée, un couloir étroit s'élargit jusqu'à se fondre dans une galerie au plafond orné d'une fine verrière.

Das Gebäude scheint wie eine Skulptur aus erstarrter Lava - seine Verkleidung aus schwarz gefärbtem Zedernholz -, die von einem üppigen Wald umgeben ist. Eine Wand durchquert den Komplex und trennt den häuslichen Bereich der Schlafzimmer. Vom Eingang aus verbreitert sich ein schmaler Gang bis zu seinem Auslaufen in einer Galerie, an deren Decke eine schmale Dachluke leuchtet.

Het gebouw lijkt op een sculptuur van gestold lava - de bekleding van zwart geverfd cederhout - en ligt beschermd in een welig bos. Een muur loopt dwars door het geheel en scheidt het leefgedeelte van de slaapkamers. Vanaf de ingang loopt een nauwe gang die breder wordt en uitkomt in een galerij waarvan het dak een smal dakraam heeft.

El edificio parece una escultura de lava solidificada –su recubrimiento de cedro teñido de negro– guarecida por un exuberante bosque. Una pared atraviesa el conjunto y divide el área doméstica de los dormitorios. Desde la entrada, un angosto pasillo se ensancha hasta morir en una galería en cuyo techo refulge un estrecho lucernario.

L'edificio sembra una scultura di lava solidificata - il rivestimento in cedro dipinto di nero - circondata da un bosco vivace. Una parete percorre diagonalmente il complesso e divide l'area domestica dalle camere. Dall'ingresso si diparte un angusto corridoio che poi confluisce in una galleria sul cui soffitto si impone uno stretto lucernario.

O edifício parece uma escultura de lava solidificada - o seu revestimento de cedro tingido de preto - adornada por um exuberante bosque. Uma parede atravessa diagonalmente o conjunto e divide a área doméstica dos quartos. A partir da entrada, um estreito corredor alarga-se até morrer numa sala em cujo tecto refulge uma estreita cobertura de vidro.

Byggnaden ser ut som en skulptur av stelnad lava, med sin beklädnad av svartbetsad ceder, och inhyses av en lummig skog. En diagonalt korsande vägg delar av helheten i hushållsrum och sovrum. Från entrén leder en smal korridor till ett galleri, där ett smalt takfönster skimrar i taket.

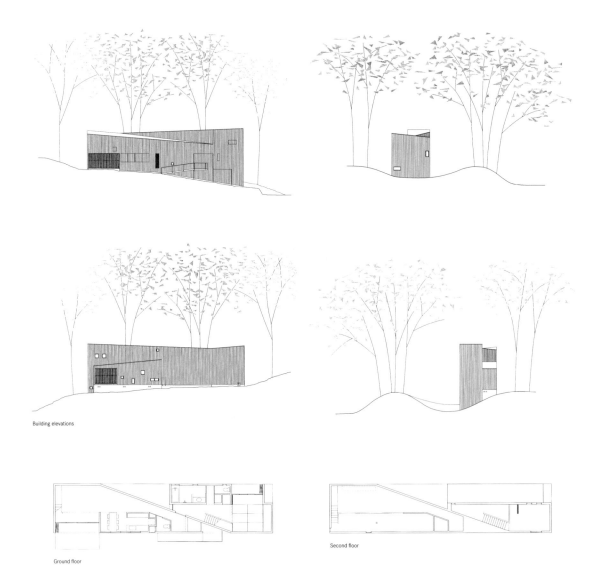

Building elevations

Ground floor

Second floor

FARMHOUSE

Jarmund/Vigsnæs
Toten, Norway
© Nils Petter Dale

The laminated wood that surrounds the building is from the adjacent farmhouse that has been demolished. Its austere interior and the surrounding window framework add light and spaciousness.

Le bois laminé qui recouvre le bâtiment provient de l'ancienne ferme annexe, aujourd'hui démolie. Son intérieur sobre – avec poutres apparentes et panneaux en contreplaqué sur les murs – et l'ensemble des fenêtres qui l'entourent – avec des vues panoramiques sur le paysage norvégien – lui confèrent clarté et espace.

Die Holzverkleidung des Hauses stammt von dem alten, nebenliegenden Bauernhof, der heute abgerissen ist. Sein schmuckloses Aussehen mit offenen Trägern und Furnierplatten, welche die Wände bedecken, sowie die umrahmende Fenstergestaltung, die Panoramablicke auf die norwegische Landschaft bietet, verleihen ihm Licht und Weite.

Het houtlaminaat waarin dit gebouw gehuld is, is afkomstig van een oude boerderij die is afgebroken. Het sobere interieur, met zichtbare balken en muren die bedekt zijn met gelaagd houten panelen, en het latwerk van ramen die deze omringt – met panoramische uitzichten over het Noorse landschap – zorgen voor licht en ruimte.

El laminado de madera que envuelve el edificio procede de la antigua granja anexa, hoy ya demolida. Su austero interior –con vigas expuestas y paneles de contrachapado cubriendo las paredes– y el entramado de ventanas que lo circunda –con vistas panorámicas sobre el paisaje noruego– le otorgan luz y amplitud.

Il laminato di legno che avvolge l'edificio proviene dall'antica fattoria annessa, attualmente demolita. Gli interni austeri – con travi a vista e pannelli di compensato che rivestono le pareti – e la serie di finestre con vista panoramica sul paesaggio norvegese trasmettono luce e senso di ampiezza.

O laminado de madeira que envolve o edifício provém da antiga quinta anexa, hoje demolida. O seu austero interior – com vigas expostas e painéis de contraplacado a cobrir as paredes – e o entramado de janelas que o circunda – com vista panorâmica sobre a paisagem norueguesa — concedem-lhe luz e amplitude.

Det laminerade virket som omsluter byggnaden kommer från den gamla intilliggande gården, idag raserad. Den spartanska interiören med sina synliga bjälkar och väggar täckta med plywoodpaneler och de omslutande fönstren med panoramautsikt över det norska landskapet ger ljus och rymd.

West elevation

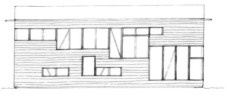

North elevation

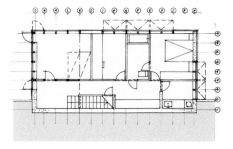

Second floor

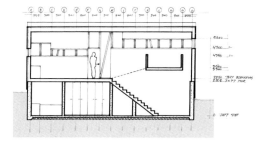

Building section

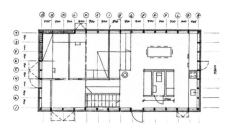

Ground floor

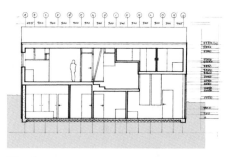

Building section

East elevation

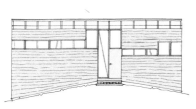

South elevation

ARKETORP VILLA

Erik Ståhl
Jönköping, Sweden
© Jan Erik Ejenstam, Erik Ståhl

The house with pure and timeless forms is organized around a central hall with two corridors connecting all the rooms. The natural environment has been preserved intact, without any intervention other than Japanese garden at the entrance. The materials celebrate the landscape: birch on walls and ceilings and ceramic floors.

La maison, de façon simple et intemporelle, s'organise autour d'un couloir central duquel émanent deux ramifications desservant toutes les pièces. L'environnement naturel a été conservé intact, avec pour seule intervention le jardin japonais à l'entrée. Les matériaux rendent hommage au paysage : du bois de bouleau sur les murs et les plafonds ; des sols en hêtre et en céramique.

Das Haus mit reinen und zeitlosen Formen ist um einen Zentralflur angeordnet, aus dem zwei Abzweigungen abgehen, die alle Zimmer verbinden. Die natürliche Umgebung blieb bis auf den japanischen Garten am Eingang intakt erhalten. Die Baumaterialien machen der Landschaft Ehre: Birke an Wänden und Decken und Böden aus Buche und Keramik.

Dit huis is, met zijn strakke en tijdloze vormen, georganiseerd rond een centrale gang van waaruit twee zijtrappen voortkomen die naar alle slaapkamers leiden. De natuurlijke omgeving is intact gelaten, met als enige inmenging de Japanse tuin bij de ingang. De materialen doen denken aan die van het landschap: berkenhout aan de muren en plafonds en beukenhout en keramiek op de vloer.

La casa, de formas puras y atemporales, se organiza en torno a un pasillo central del cual emanan dos ramales que conectan todas las habitaciones. El entorno natural se ha preservado intacto, sin más intervención que el jardín japonés de la entrada. Los materiales festejan el paisaje: abedul en paredes y techos y suelos de haya y cerámica.

La casa, dalle forme pure e atemporali, è organizzata intorno a un corridoio centrale dal quale si dipartono due passaggi che mettono in comunicazione tutte le camere. Il contesto naturale è rimasto intatto, salvo l'intervento per la realizzazione del giardino giapponese dell'ingresso. I materiali sono una celebrazione del paesaggio: betulla su pareti e soffitti, pavimento di faggio e ceramica.

A casa, de formas puras e intemporais, organiza-se em torno a um corredor central do qual derivam dois ramais que ligam todas as divisões. O ambiente natural preservou-se intacto, sem mais intervenção do que o jardim japonês da entrada. Os materiais festejam a paisagem: bétula em paredes e tectos e pavimentos de faia e cerâmica.

Huset med sina rena och tidlösa former är organiserat kring en central korridor med två sidogångar som förenar alla rum. Den naturliga omgivningen har bevarats intakt utan andra ingrepp än den japanska trädgården vid entrén. Materialen hyllar landskapet - väggar av björk och golv av bok och keramik.

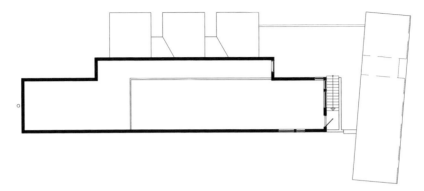

Second floor

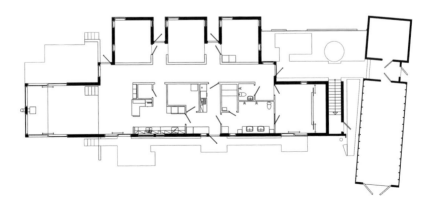

Ground floor

Building section

GARDEN STUDIO **MONO**

Ecospace
Mobile
© Ecospace

The prefabricated modules by Ecospace® are an affordable and ecological alternative to add spaces in gardens and terraces. There are a variety of customizable models, dimensions and properties. Built with cedar wood, they have underfloor heating, lighting, SIP panels and, optionally, a green roof.

Les modules préfabriqués Ecospace® constituent une alternative accessible et écologique pour ajouter des espaces sur les terrasses et jardins. Il en existe différents modèles, de dimensions et caractéristiques personnalisables. Fabriqués en bois de cèdre, ils disposent d'un chauffage au sol, de l'éclairage et d'un revêtement en panneaux SIP, mais également - en option - d'une toiture végétale.

Die fertigen Ecospace® Module sind eine erschwingliche und ökologische Alternative, um Räumlichkeiten in Gärten und auf Terrassen hinzuzufügen. Es gibt eine Vielfalt an Modellen mit anpassbaren Abmessungen und Eigenschaften. Sie sind aus Zedernholz gebaut, verfügen über Fußbodenheizung, Beleuchtung, SIP-Paneelverkleidung und optional auch über Pflanzdach.

De voorgefabriceerde modules van Ecospace® zijn een toegankelijk en milieuvriendelijk alternatief om ruimtes toe te voegen aan tuinen en terrassen. Er bestaan verschillende modellen, afmetingen en eigenschappen die op maat kunnen worden gemaakt. Ze zijn vervaardigd uit cederhout, beschikken over vloerverwarming, verlichting, bekleding met SIP panelen en optioneel over een begroeid dak.

Los módulos prefabricados de Ecospace® son una alternativa asequible y ecológica para añadir espacios en jardines y terrazas. Existe una gran variedad de modelos, de dimensiones y propiedades personalizables. Construidos con madera de cedro, disponen de calefacción bajo el suelo, iluminación, recubrimiento de paneles SIP y, opcionalmente, tejado vegetal.

I moduli prefabbricati Ecospace® rappresentano un'alternativa accessibile ed ecologica per aggiungere spazi a giardini e terrazze. Sono disponibili vari modelli, di dimensioni e caratteristiche personalizzabili. Realizzati in legno di cedro, dispongono di riscaldamento a pavimento, illuminazione, rivestimento con pannelli SIP e, in via opzionale, tetto vegetale.

Os módulos prefabricados de Ecospace® são uma alternativa exequível e ecológica para acrescentar espaços em jardins e terraços. Existe uma grande variedade de modelos, de dimensões e propriedades personalizáveis. Construídos com madeira de cedro, dispõem de aquecimento de pavimento, iluminação, revestimento de painéis SIP e - opcionalmente - telhado vegetal.

Ecospace® prefabricerade moduler utgör ett prisvärt och ekologiskt alternativ för att addera rum i trädgårdar och på terrasser. De finns i olika beställningsbara modeller, dimensioner och med olika egenskaper. De är tillverkade av cederträ och har golvvärme, belysning, SIP-panelbeklädning och, om så önskas, växttak.

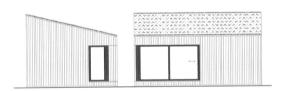

Building elevations

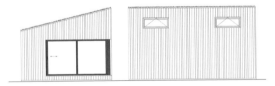

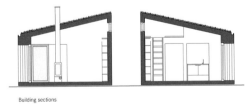

Building sections

Floor plan and mezzanine level

HÖLICK SEA RESORT

Mats Edlund, Henrietta Palmer, Matts Ingman
Hudiksvall, Sweden
© Jacob Nordström

Housing built entirely of wood. The roof – designed as a *faltak* or sloping roof characteristic of the island of Gotland in the Baltic – and wooden façades give it the appearance of a cabin hidden among the pines. The interior, compact yet diaphanous, is enough to house everything you need in a summer house in Sweden.

Logement intégralement fabriqué en bois. Son toit – façon *faltak* ou toiture inclinée caractéristique de l'île de Gotland, en mer Baltique – et ses façades en bois lui donnent l'allure d'une cabane dissimulée dans le bois de pins. L'intérieur, compact bien que diaphane, est suffisant pour héberger tout le nécessaire d'une maison de vacances suédoise.

Vollständig aus Holz erbautes Haus. Das Dach im Stil eines *faltak* oder der für die Ostseeinsel Gotland charakteristischen Schrägdächer, wie auch die Holzfassaden verleihen dem Haus den Eindruck einer im Kiefernwald versteckten Hütte. Der kompakte aber leere Innenraum reicht aus, um alles bergen zu können, was ein schwedisches Sommerhaus braucht.

Geheel uit hout opgetrokken woning. Het dak is een *faltak*: een schuin dak dat kenmerkend is voor het eiland Gotland in de Oostzee, en de houten gevels geven hem het uiterlijk van een in het dennenbos verscholen hut. In het compacte doch heldere interieur is voldoende ruimte voor alles wat nodig is in een Zweeds zomerhuis.

Vivienda construida íntegramente con madera. El tejado, a modo de *faltak* o techumbre inclinada característica de la isla de Gotland, en el Báltico, y las fachadas de madera imprimen la apariencia de una cabaña oculta entre el pinar. El interior, compacto aunque diáfano, es suficiente para acoger todo lo necesario en una casa de veraneo sueca.

Abitazione costruita interamente in legno. Il tetto – tipo *faltak* o copertura inclinata caratteristica dell'isola di Gotland, nel Baltico – e le facciate in legno conferiscono alla struttura l'aspetto di una capanna nascosta nella pineta. Gli interni, compatti ma luminosi, sono sufficienti a contenere tutto ciò che serve in una casa di vacanze svedese.

Moradia construída integramente com madeira. O telhado – ao estilo de *faltak* ou telhado inclinado característica da ilha de Gotlândia, no Báltico – e as fachadas de madeira conferem-lhe a aparência de uma cabana escondida entre o pinhal. O interior, compacto ainda que diáfano, é suficiente para acolher tudo o necessário numa casa de verão sueca.

Bostad byggd helt i trä. Taket, ett *faltak* eller sluttande tak kännetecknande för ön Gotland i Östersjön, och väggarna i trä gör att den ser ut som en stuga gömd bland tallarna. Insidan är kompakt med ändå öppen och räcker till för att rymma allt som behövs i en sommarbostad i Sverige.

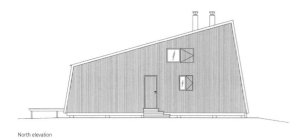

North elevation

West elevation

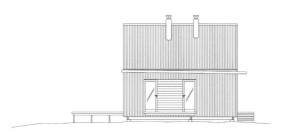

East elevation

South elevation

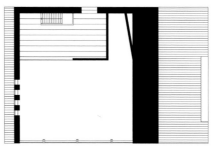

Attic

Ground floor

MACKILSTON HOUSE

Simon Winstanley Architects
Dalry, United Kingdom
© Simon Winstanley Architects

The project is governed by criteria of ecology and efficiency. The lightweight steel and insulating wood frame and zinc-plated roof prevent heat loss. The gap between the roofs makes room for a strip of skylights providing constant insulation. The solar panels, windmill and water collector guarantee self-sufficiency.

Le projet est régi par des critères précis d'écologie et d'efficacité. L'armature légère en acier et en bois isolant, de même que la toiture recouverte de zinc, préviennent la perte de chaleur. L'écart entre les toitures laisse la place à une bande de lucarnes qui permettent un ensoleillement continu. Les panneaux solaires, le moulin et le collecteur d'eau de pluie assurent l'autosuffisance du bâtiment.

Das Projekt richtet sich nach Ökologie- und Effizienzkriterien. Das leichte Gerüst aus Stahl und isolierendem Holz, wie auch das verzinkte Dach beugen Wärmeverlust vor. Der Höhenunterschied zwischen den Dächern lässt einen Streifen Dachluken frei, sodass eine ständige Sonnenbestrahlung möglich ist. Solarpaneele, eine kleine Mühle und die Wasserauffangvorrichtung gewährleisten seine Selbstgenügsamkeit.

Het project wordt geregeld door criteria van ecologie en efficiëntie. De lichte draagconstructie van staal en isolerend hout en het verzinkte dak gaan warmteverlies tegen. Door het hoogteverschil tussen de daken komt een strook dakramen vrij, waardoor continu zonlicht naar binnen kan schijnen. De zonnepanelen, het molentje en wateropvangsysteem garanderen zelfvoorziening.

El proyecto se rige por criterios de ecología y eficiencia. El ligero armazón de acero y madera aislante y el tejado bañado en zinc previenen la pérdida de calor. El desnivel entre cubiertas libera una franja de tragaluces que permite una insolación continua. Los paneles solares, el molinillo y el recolector de aguas garantizan su autosuficiencia.

Il progetto si basa su criteri di efficienza e sostenibilità ambientale. Il leggero telaio di acciaio e legno isolante e il tetto impregnato di zinco evitano la perdita di calore. Il dislivello tra i tetti crea una seria di lucernari che garantiscono un irraggiamento continuo. I pannelli solari, il piccolo aerogeneratore e il sistema di raccolta dell'acqua garantiscono l'autosufficienza della struttura.

O projecto rege-se por critérios de ecologia e eficiência. A leve armação de aço e madeira isolante e o telhado banhado a zinco impedem a perda de calor. O desnível entre coberturas liberta uma faixa de clarabóias que permite uma exposição solar contínua. Os painéis solares, o moinho e o recolector de águas garantem a sua auto-suficiência.

Projektet regleras av kriterier för ekologi och effektivitet. Den lätta ramen av stål och isolerande trä samt det förzinkade taket förhindrar värmeförluster. Olika takhöjder skapar en fri rännil med takfönster som ger ständig insolation. Solpaneler, vindkraftverk och vattenkollektor säkerställer självförsörjningen.

North elevation – entrance

West elevation – front

South elevation

East elevation – rear

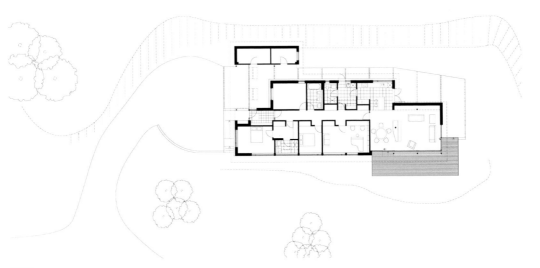

Floor plan

HÄFENBERG HOUSE

Gerold Wiederin
Dornbirn, Austria
© A.T. Neubau

In order to exalt the view over the valley and supply natural light, the building was positioned on top of a slope. The glass exterior of the east and west façades contrasts with the opacity of the north and south. The exterior brick walls are covered with a mineral mixture that gives the building its unique gray tone.

Afin d'exploiter au maximum la vue sur la vallée et la lumière naturelle, le bâtiment a été érigé au sommet d'une pente. L'enveloppe en verre des façades est et ouest contraste avec l'opacité des côtés nord et sud. Ses murs extérieurs en briques sont recouverts d'un mélange minéral qui donne au bâtiment sa teinte cendrée particulière.

Um den Blick auf das Tal zu betonen und Tageslicht zu erhalten, liegt das Gebäude auf dem Gipfel eines Abhangs. Die Glasumhüllung der Ost- und Westfassade steht mit der Undurchlässigkeit der Nord- und Südbereiche im Kontrast. Seine Backsteinaußenwände sind mit einer mineralischen Mischung bedeckt, die dem Gebäude seines besonderen aschgrauen Ton verleiht.

Teneinde het uitzicht over de vallei te benadrukken en het nodige hemellicht binnen te laten, is het gebouw op de top van een heuvel geplaatst. De gazen bekleding van de oost- en westgevel contrasteert met de opaciteit van de noord- en zuidkant. De bakstenen buitenmuren zijn bedekt met een mengsel van mineralen dat het gebouw zijn bijzondere askleurige tint geeft.

A fin de exaltar la vista sobre el valle y abastecerse de luz natural, el edificio se aposta en la cima de una pendiente. La envoltura de cristal de las fachadas este y oeste contrasta con la opacidad de los lados norte y sur. Sus paredes exteriores de ladrillo están cubiertas de una mezcla mineral que da al edificio su particular tono ceniciento.

Per godere della vista sulla vallata e ottenere luce naturale, l'edificio è ubicato sulla cima di un dislivello. Le facciate est e ovest ricoperte da vetrate contrastano con l'opacità del lato nord e sud. Le pareti esterne a mattoni sono rivestite da una miscela a base di minerali che conferisce all'edificio un particolare tono cenerino.

Com a finalidade de exaltar a vista sobre o vale e abastecer-se de luz natural, o edifício assenta no cimo de uma encosta. A envoltura de vidro das fachadas este e oeste contrasta com a opacidade dos lados norte e sul. As suas paredes exteriores de tijolo estão cobertas por uma mistura mineral que dá ao edifício o seu particular tom cinzento.

För att förhöja utsikten över dalen och bada i naturligt ljus uppfördes byggnaden på toppen av en sluttning. Väster- och österväggarnas glashölje kontrasterar mot norr- och södersidornas ogenomskinlighet. Ytterväggarna av tegel är täckta med en mineralblandning som ger byggnaden dess unika grå ton.

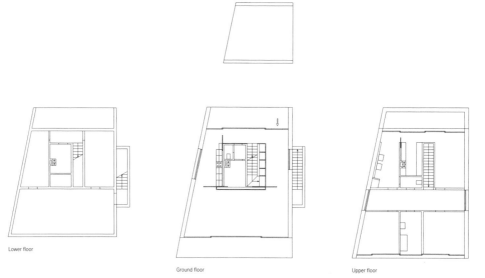

Lower floor

Ground floor

Upper floor

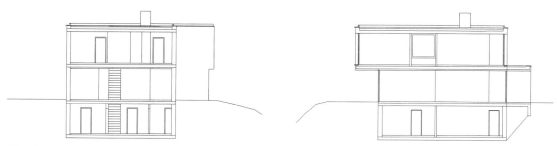

Building sections

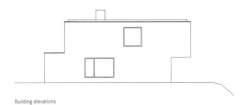

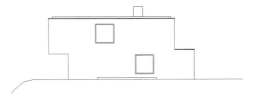

Building elevations

Building elevations

FLOWING LAKE RESIDENCE

David Vandervort Architects
Snohomish, WA, USA
© Mark Woods Photography

The house attempts to discreetly rest on the site. Perched on the steep hill, on its west façade, the balconies, NanaWall® windows and a terrace elevated above the trees convert it into a lookout over the lake, its vanishing point. The wooden sides fuse the disinhibition of the west wing with the intimacy of the woodland of the entrance façade.

La maison aspire à une intégration discrète dans son environnement. Perchée sur la colline, avec des balcons orientés à l'ouest, des murs de verre NanaWall® et une terrasse dominant la cime des arbres, elle s'élève telle une tour de guet au-dessus du lac, son point de fuite. Ses façades en bois relient l'ouverture de l'aile ouest à l'intimité arborescente de la façade d'accès.

Das Haus versucht, sich diskret an seinem Ort einzufügen. Am steilen Abhang angesiedelt, verwandelt es sich mit seinen Balkonen an der Westfassade, den NanaWall® Fenstern und einer Terrasse über den Bäumen zu einem Aussichtsturm über den See und Fluchtpunkt. Die Seiten aus Holz verbinden die Freizügigkeit des Westflügels mit der Vertrautheit der Bäume der Zugangsfassade.

Het huis heeft de bedoeling om zich discreet op de locatie te implanteren. Het is verrezen op de steile helling en heeft op de westgevel balkons, NanaWall® beglazing en een terras dat boven de bomen verheven is. Dit maakt van de woning een uitkijktoren over het meer, zijn vluchtpunt. De houten zijkanten verbinden de onbelemmerdheid van de westvleugel met de intimiteit van de hoofdgevel.

La casa busca implantarse discretamente en el lugar. Encaramada en la inclinada cuesta, en su fachada oeste balcones, cristaleras NanaWall® y una terraza elevada sobre los árboles hacen de ella una atalaya sobre el lago, su punto de fuga. Los laterales de madera engarzan la desinhibición del ala oste con la intimidad arbórea de su fachada de acceso.

La casa mira a inserirsi discretamente nel contesto. Appoggiata su un dislivello, la casa nella facciata ovest è arricchita da balconi, vetrate NanaWall® e una terrazza rialzata sugli alberi che ne fanno una sorta di torre di vedetta sul lago, il suo punto di fuga. Gli elementi laterali in legno coniugano la rilassatezza dell'ala ovest con l'intimità arborea della facciata di ingresso.

A casa procura implantar-se discretamente no local. Empoleirada na inclinada encosta, na sua fachada oeste varandas, vidraças NanaWall® e um terraço elevado sobre as árvores fazem dele uma atalaia sobre o lago, o seu ponto de fuga. Os laterais de madeira encaixam a desinibição da ala oeste com a intimidade arbórea da sua fachada de acesso.

Huset söker diskret etablera sig på platsen. Det är beläget högt upp på den branta sluttningen och har balkonger på västerväggen, NanaWall®-fönster och en upphöjd terrass över träden vilket gör det till en utsiktspost över sjön, dess flyktpunkt. Sidorna av trä förankrar den västra vingens hämningar med träets förtrolighet med entréväggen.

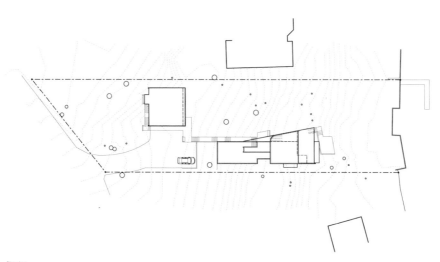

Site plan

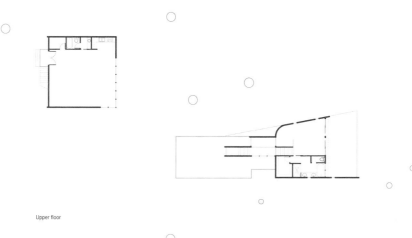

Upper floor

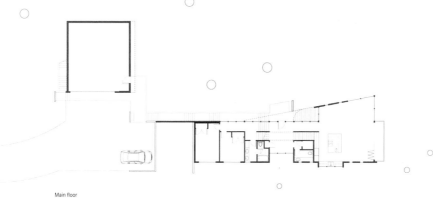

Main floor

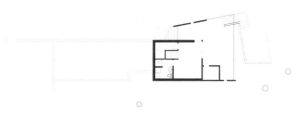

Lower floor

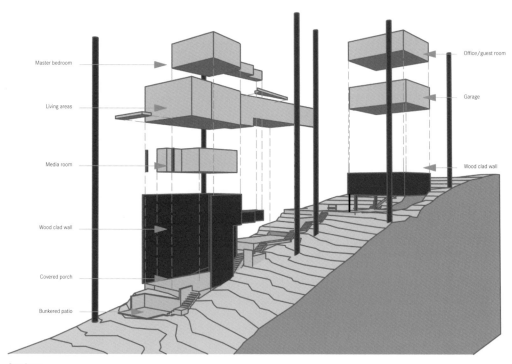

Master bedroom

Living areas

Media room

Wood clad wall

Covered porch

Bunkered patio

Office / guest room

Garage

Wood clad wall

Room diagram

ENGLISH RESIDENCE

ZeroEnergy Design
Orleans, MA, USA
© ZeroEnergy Design

Three units of geometry and different materials shape the space: in the basement, a red box contains the kitchen and living room, an orange box, the bedrooms and bathrooms, and on the second floor, a cedar box holds the main bedroom and studio. The pebble entrance path identifies the presence of vibrant fall colors of the façade.

Trois unités, de géométrie et matériaux différents, donnent forme à l'ensemble : en bas, un module rouge (cuisine et pièce à vivre) et un autre orange (chambres et salles de bains) ; en haut, un module en cèdre (chambre principale et bureau). Le chemin de galets à l'entrée fait ressortir le ton automnal ardent de la façade.

Drei unterschiedliche geometrische Einheiten und Baumaterialien geben dem Ganzen Form: Unten, ein roter Kasten mit Küche und Wohnzimmer und ein orangener Kasten für Schlafzimmer und Bäder. Auf der zweiten Etage ein Zedernkasten mit Elternschlafzimmer und Studio. Der Kieselpfad des Eingangs unterstreicht die kraftvollen Herbstfarbtöne der Fassade.

Drie eenheden met verschillende geometrie en materialen geven het geheel vorm: op de benedenverdieping bevindt zich een rode kubus met de keuken en eetkamer en een oranje kubus voor de slaapkamers en badkamers; op de tweede verdieping omvat een cederhouten doos de hoofdslaapkamer en studeerkamer. Het pad van kiezelstenen naar de ingang benadrukt de aanwezigheid van de levendige herfstkleuren van de gevel.

Tres unidades de geometría y materiales distintos dan forma al conjunto: en los bajos, una caja roja, con la cocina y la sala de estar, y otra naranja, con los dormitorios y los baños; en la segunda planta, una caja de cedro, con el dormitorio principal y el estudio–. El sendero de guijarros de la entrada subraya la presencia de los vibrantes tonos otoñales de la fachada.

Tre unità con geometria e materiali diversi danno forma all'insieme: al piano terra una scatola rossa con cucina e salotto e un'altra arancione con camere e bagni; al secondo piano una scatola di cedro con camera principale e studio. Il sentiero di ghiaia all'ingresso sottolinea la presenza dei vivaci toni autunnali della facciata.

Três unidades de geometria e materiais distintos dão forma ao conjunto: em baixo, uma caixa vermelha – cozinha e sala de estar – e outra laranja – quartos e casas de banho –; no segundo piso, uma caixa de cedro – quarto principal e estúdio. O caminho de seixos da entrada sublinha a presença dos vibrantes tons outonais da fachada.

Tre enheter av olika geometri och material formar helheten. Nertill, en röd låda med kök och vardagsrum och en orange låda med sovrum och badrum. På andra plan, en låda av cederträ med det stora sovrummet samt arbetsrum. Vägen med kiselsten vid entrén betonar fasadens livfulla höstfärger.

Second floor

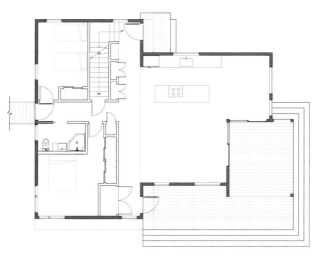

Ground floor

CLIFF HOUSE

Altius Architecture
Muskoka Lakes, Canada
© Jonathan Savoie

The areas of the house pivot around a central space trapping and distributing light and air. Mitigating the robustness of the two stone chimneys, the overhangs and glass façade project it towards the lake. The pine cladding and Douglas fir wood used for the exterior woodwork make references to the landscape and protect the estate from the severe climate.

Les espaces de la maison s'agencent autour d'une ouverture centrale qui capte et répartit l'air et la lumière. Contrastant avec la robustesse des deux cheminées de pierre, les saillies et le verre de la façade la projettent vers le lac. Le revêtement en pin et en sapin de Douglas utilisé pour la charpente extérieure rappelle le paysage alentour et protège la propriété du climat rude.

Die Bereiche des Hauses drehen sich um eine zentrale Öffnung, die Licht und Luft auffängt und sie verteilt. Die Auskragungen und das Glas der Fassade mildern die Robustheit der beiden Steinkamine und orientieren das Haus Richtung See. Die Verkleidung aus Kiefer und die Außentüren und -fenster aus Douglas-Tannenholz erinnern an die Landschaft und schützen den Grundbesitz vor dem strengen Klima.

De vertrekken van het huis draaien om een centrale opening die licht en lucht vangt en verdeelt. De forsheid van de twee stenen schoorstenen wordt verzacht door uitspringende delen en het glas van de gevel projecteren het in de richting van het meer. De bekleding van grenenhouten en Douglassparren, die gebruikt is voor de kozijnen buiten, verwijzen naar het landschap en beschermen de woning tegen het strenge klimaat.

Los espacios de la casa pivotan en torno a un hueco central que atrapa y distribuye la luz y el aire. Mitigando la robustez de las dos chimeneas de piedra, los voladizos y el cristal de la fachada la proyectan hacia el lago. El recubrimiento de pino y la madera de abeto de Douglas usada para la carpintería exterior remiten al paisaje y protegen a la finca del severo clima.

Gli spazi della casa ruotano intorno a un'apertura centrale che cattura e distribuisce la luce e l'aria. Smorzando la robustezza dei due camini in pietra, gli elementi sospesi e il vetro della facciata proiettano la struttura verso il lago. Il rivestimento di pino e il legno di abete di Douglas utilizzati per la parte esterna richiamano il paesaggio e proteggono la struttura dal clima rigido.

Os espaços da casa giram em torno a um vão central que apanha e distribui a luz e o ar. Mitigando a robustez das duas chaminés de pedra, as palas e o vidro da fachada projectam-na para o lago. O revestimento de pinho e a madeira de abeto de Douglas usada para a carpintaria exterior encaminham para a paisagem e protegem a quinta do severo clima.

Husets utrymmen roterar kring ett hål i mitten där ljus och luft fångas upp och fördelas. Utsprången och glasfasaden mildrar robustheten i de två skorstenarna av sten, och riktar huset mot sjön. Beklädnaden av furu och yttre snickerier av douglasgrantrå hänvisar till landskapet och skyddar egendomen mot hårt väder.

Site plan

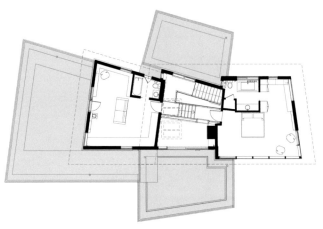

Second floor

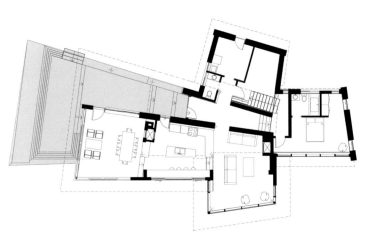

Ground floor

CABIN NEARBY **STAVANGER**

Gudmundur Jonsson Arkitektkontor
Stavanger, Norway
© Jiri Havran

The cottage, designed for mass production adapts to any potential environment. The interior layout distinguishes activity areas from rest areas. Surrounding both areas, a glass curtain gives the home the look of a pavilion with sliding doors. The roof and terrace, designed as a unit, reinforce this idea.

La cabane, conçue pour être fabriquée en série, s'adapte à toutes sortes d'environnements. L'agencement intérieur sépare les zones d'activités et celles de repos. Un rideau de verre encercle les deux espaces et confère à l'ensemble une allure de pavillon aux portes coulissantes. Le toit et la terrasse, conçus comme une unité, viennent renforcer cette idée.

Die Hütte, die für serienmäßige Nachbildungen gedacht ist, passt sich allen möglichen Umgebungen an. Die Innenaufteilung trennt Arbeitsbereiche von Entspannungsbereichen. Ein Glasvorhang, der beide Bereiche umgibt, verleiht dem Komplex das Aussehen eines Pavillons mit Schiebetüren. Dach und Terrasse, die als Einheit gedacht sind, verstärken diesen Eindruck.

De hut, die bedoeld is om in serie te worden gereproduceerd, past zich aan iedere mogelijke omgeving aan. De indeling van binnen scheidt de leefruimte af van de rustzones. Een glazen gordijn, die beide zones omringt, geeft het geheel het uiterlijk van een paviljoen met schuifdeuren. Dak en terras, die als een eenheid zijn bedacht versterken dat idee.

La cabaña, pensada para ser reproducida en serie, se adapta a cualquier entorno posible. La distribución interior discrimina las áreas de actividad de las de descanso. Rodeando a ambas, una cortina de cristal da al conjunto el aspecto de un pabellón con puertas correderas. Tejado y terraza, concebidos como una unidad, refuerzan esta idea.

La capanna, progettata per essere riprodotta in serie, si adatta a qualsiasi contesto. La distribuzione interna suddivide le aree dedicate alle attività da quelle di riposo. Una parete di vetro circonda entrambe dando al complesso l'aspetto di un padiglione con porte scorrevoli. Tetto e terrazza, concepiti come una sola unità, rafforzano questa idea.

A cabana, pensada para ser reproduzida em série, adapta-se a qualquer ambiente possível. A distribuição interior discrimina as áreas de actividade das de descanso. Rodeando ambas, uma cortina de vidro dá ao conjunto o aspecto de um pavilhão com portas deslizantes. Telhado e terraço, concebidos como uma unidade, reforçam esta ideia.

Stugan är tänkt att framställas i serie och anpassar sig efter alla möjliga miljöer. Interiören separerar aktivitetsutrymmen från viloutrymmen. En glasgardin omger båda, och ger det hela ett utseende av paviljong med skjutdörrar. Tak och terrass, utformade som en helhet, förstärker denna idé.

Floor plan

LINGG HOUSE

Dietrich + Untertrifaller Architekten
Bregenz, Austria
© Ignacio Martínez

The setback on the second floor allows for a balcony in the attic and projects an overhang over the entrance. The common areas are upstairs. In the middle, with access to garden, there are the bedrooms, and the basement houses the garage and storage area. The concrete volume, bordered with metal and plywood, is totally integrated into the landscape..

Le retrait du deuxième étage laisse la place pour un balcon au dernier étage et projette une saillie au-dessus de l'entrée. Les espaces communs se trouvent au dernier étage ; les chambres occupent le rez-de-chaussée, avec un accès au jardin ; le sous-sol, quant à lui, héberge le garage et le cellier. Son corps en béton, bordé de métal et contreplaqué, s'impose avec force dans le paysage.

Die zurückgesetzte zweite Etage lässt Raum für einen Balkon im Dachgeschoss und legt eine Auskragung über den Eingang. Im Obergeschoss befinden sich die Gemeinschaftsbereiche, in der Mitte, mit Zugang zum Garten, die Schlafzimmer, und im Untergeschoss liegen Garage und Lager. Das mit Metall und Furnier umrahmte Betongerüst hebt sich deutlich über die Landschaft hervor.

De terugspringing van de tweede verdieping laat ruimte over voor een balkon op de zolderverdieping en zorgt voor een uitstekend gedeelte boven de ingang. Op de bovenverdieping bevinden zich de gemeenschappelijke ruimtes; op de tussenverdieping is de toegang tot de tuin en zijn de slaapkamers te vinden, en in het souterrain bevinden zich de garage en opslagruimte. Het betonnen hoofdbestanddeel met metalen en gelaagd houten afwerkband staat stevig in het landschap.

El retranqueo de la segunda planta deja sitio a un balcón en el ático y proyecta un voladizo sobre la entrada. En la planta superior están las zonas comunes; en medio, con acceso al jardín, los dormitorios; el sótano aloja el garaje y el almacén. Su cuerpo de hormigón, ribeteado de metal y contrachapado, se afirma rotundamente sobre el paisaje.

La rientranza del secondo piano lascia spazio a un balcone sull'attico e crea un elemento sospeso sopra l'ingresso. Al piano superiore troviamo le aree comuni; nel mezzo, con accesso al giardino, le camere; il seminterrato ospita il garage e il magazzino. Il corpo in cemento armato, rifinito in metallo e compensato, si impone in modo chiaro sul paesaggio.

O segundo andar recuado deixa espaço a uma varanda no sótão e projecta uma pala sobre a entrada. No piso superior encontram-se as zonas comuns; ao meio, com acesso ao jardim, os quartos; a cave aloja a garagem e a arrecadação. O seu corpo de betão, debruado de metal e contraplacado, afirma-se rotundamente sobre a paisagem.

Andra våningens avbräck ger rum åt en balkong på vinden och projicerar ett utsprång över entrén. På övervåningen finns de gemensamma utrymmena, på mellanplan och med utgång till trädgården ligger sovrummen, och i källaren hyses garage och förråd. Betongkroppen, kantad av metall och plywood, hävdar sig kategoriskt i landskapet.

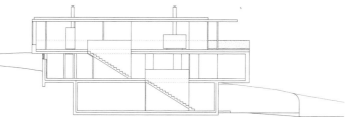

Building section

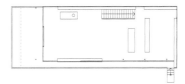

Third floor

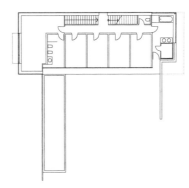

Second floor

Ground floor

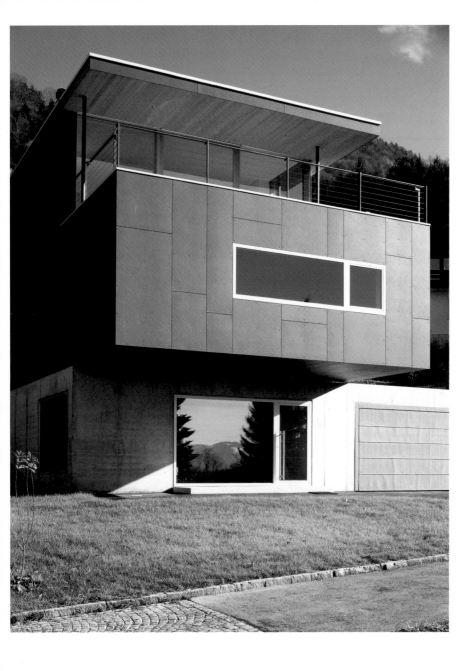

VILLA **HÅKANSSON**

Johan Sundberg
Höllviken, Sweden
© Kasper Dudzik

The house, arranged around a courtyard to honor the Danish tradition of the 1960s and 1970s, contains the bedroom on the north and leaves the west, with the most sunshine, to the areas of activity. A Pedersen brick shell, the Schüco aluminum used in the sliding doors and oak façade and garage hide their wood and steel frame.

Dans la maison agencée autour d'un atrium, conformément à la tradition danoise des années 1960 et 1970, les chambres sont situées dans l'aile nord tandis que la partie ouest, plus ensoleillée, est réservée aux zones d'activités. Une charpente en briques Pedersen, l'aluminium Schüco des portes coulissantes et le bois de chêne de la façade et du garage dissimulent son armature en bois et en acier.

Das Haus ist nach dänischer Tradition der 60er und 70er Jahre um einen Innenhof angeordnet. Die Schlafzimmer liegen im Nordflügel und lassen den Westflügel mit der höheren Sonneneinstrahlung für die Arbeitsbereiche. Ein Gehäuse aus Pedersen Backsteinen, Schiebetüren aus Schüco-Aluminium, Fassade aus Eiche und die Garage verstecken sein Gerüst aus Holz und Stahl.

Het huis, dat is vormgegeven rond een voorhof die de Deense traditie van de jaren 60 en 70 eer aandoet, heeft de slaapkamers in de noordvleugel, terwijl de leefgedeeltes zich in de westzijde bevinden, waar de meeste zon komt. Een Pedersen stenen geraamte, Schüco aluminium in de schuifdeuren en eikenhout op de gevel en de garage verbergen de houten en stalen draagconstructie.

La casa, dispuesta en torno a un atrio en honor a la tradición danesa de los años sesenta y setenta, fija sus dormitorios en el ala norte y deja en la oeste, la de mayor insolación, sus áreas de actividad. Una carcasa de ladrillos Pedersen, el aluminio Schüco de las puertas correderas y el roble de la fachada y el garaje ocultan su armazón de madera y acero.

La casa, disposta intorno a un atrio nel rispetto della tradizione danese degli anni '60 e '70, ha le camere nell'ala nord lasciando alla zona ovest, quella maggiormente illuminata dal sole, gli ambienti dedicati alle attività. Una struttura a mattoni Pedersen, l'alluminio Schüco delle porte scorrevoli, il rovere della facciata e il garage nascondono il telaio di legno e acciaio.

A casa, disposta em torno a um átrio em honra à tradição dinamarquesa dos anos 60 e 70, fixa os seus quartos na ala norte e deixa na oeste, a de maior exposição solar, as suas áreas de actividade. Uma estrutura de tijolos Pedersen, o alumínio Schüco das portas deslizantes e o carvalho da fachada e a garagem ocultam a sua armação de madeira e aço.

Hemmet har arrangerats runt en förgård för att hedra den danska traditionen från 60- och 70-talet. Sovrummen är belägna i norra vingen och aktivitetsutrymmen i den västra, den med mest solljus. Ett hölje av Pedersons tegel, Schücos skjutdörrar i aluminium och fasader och garage av ekträ döljer stommen av trä och stål.

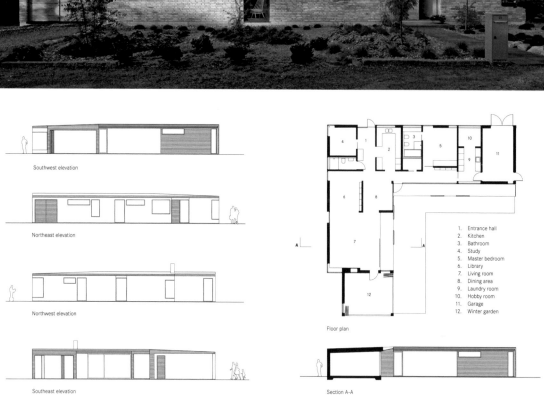

Southwest elevation

Northeast elevation

Northwest elevation

Southeast elevation

Floor plan

1. Entrance hall
2. Kitchen
3. Bathroom
4. Study
5. Master bedroom
6. Library
7. Living room
8. Dining area
9. Laundry room
10. Hobby room
11. Garage
12. Winter garden

A

A

Section A-A

8 X 8 HOUSE

Marià Castelló
Eïvissa, Spain
© Lourdes Grivé, Marià Castelló

The task was to add a self-sufficient annex to the house with only two conditions: preserving the vegetation of the area and adapting to the existing building. The resulting volume, an 8 x 8 plan with public spaces, dining room and kitchen, in the form of lobbies, attempts to gain usable space with minimal intervention.

La commande consistait à augmenter la surface de la maison au moyen d'une annexe auto-suffisante, avec deux conditions à respecter : conserver la végétation du lieu et s'adapter à l'édifice préexistant. La volumétrie obtenue, un plan de 8 x 8 avec des espaces publiques – pièce à vivre, salle à manger et cuisine – faisant office de vestibule, aspire à gagner de la surface utile avec une intervention minimale.

Der Auftrag lautete, das Haus mit einem eigenständigen Anbau unter zwei Bedingungen zu erweitern: Die Vegetation des Ortes zu erhalten und sich an das bestehende Gebäude anzupassen. Die entstandene Volumetrie – eine 8 x 8 m große Etage mit öffentlichen Bereichen wie Wohnzimmer, Esszimmer und Küche als Verteiler – versucht, Nutzfläche mit einem Mindestumbau zu gewinnen.

De opdracht bestond uit het uitbreiden van het huis door middel van een zelfvoorzienend bijgebouw, waarin moest worden voldaan aan twee voorwaarden: het behoud van de begroeiing van de plaats en het aanpassen aan het vooraf bestaande gebouw. Met het daaruit voortkomende volume, een grondvlak van 8 x 8 met openbare ruimtes—zitkamer, eetkamer en keuken, is getracht om bruikbare ruimte te winnen met minimale inmenging.

El encargo consistía en ampliar la casa mediante un anexo autosuficiente con dos condiciones: conservar la vegetación del lugar y amoldarse al edificio preexistente. La volumetría resultante, una planta de 8 x 8 con espacios públicos –estar, comedor y cocina– a modo de distribuidores, trata de ganar espacio útil con una intervención mínima.

L'incarico prevedeva l'ampiamento della casa tramite la realizzazione di un annesso autosufficiente, rispettando due condizioni: preservare la vegetazione del luogo e rifarsi all'edificio preesistente. La volumetria risultante, una pianta di 8 x 8 con zone comuni distribuite – salotto, tinello e cucina – mirano a conquistare spazio utile con un intervento minimo.

A encomenda consistia em ampliar a casa através de um anexo autossuficiente sob duas condições: conservar a vegetação do local e moldar-se ao edifício preexistente. A volumetria resultante, uma planta de 8 x 8 com espaços públicos – sala de convívio, de jantar e cozinha – do tipo de distribuidores, trata de ganhar espaço útil com uma intervenção mínima.

Uppdraget bestod i att bygga ut huset med hjälp av ett självständigt annex inom ramen för två villkor: platsens växtlighet skulle bevaras och man skulle anpassa sig efter den befintliga byggnaden. De resulterande rummen på ett våningsplan på 8 x 8 använder sig av de gemensamma utrymmena, vardagsrum, matsal och kök, som genomgångsrum och söker på så vis vinna användbart utrymme med minsta möjliga ingrepp.

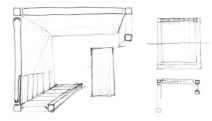

Preliminary sketches

CASA **DEL BOSQUE**

Gonzalez Vergara Arquitectos (formerly F3 Arquitectos)
Cachagua, Chile
© Ignacio Infante

The program's goal is to create multifunctional spaces in a building that takes root in the surrounding forest. To minimize its footprint on the environment, using local materials or avoiding cutting trees or modifying the slope on which the building sits, nature seems to comfortably slip inside and settle on the interior of the construction.

L'objectif du programme est de créer des espaces multifonctionnels dans un édifice en l'intégrant à la forêt qui l'entoure. En minimisant son impact sur l'environnement – au moyen de matériaux indigènes, en évitant de couper des arbres ou de modifier la pente sous le bâtiment –, la nature semble se faufiler à l'intérieur et s'y installer confortablement.

Das Ziel des Programms lautete, Mehrzweckräume in einem Gebäude zu erstellen, das Wurzeln in dem umgebenden Wald zu ziehen scheint. Indem es seine Spuren in der Landschaft anhand der Verwendung bodenständiger Materialien, der Vermeidung des Baumfällens oder der Beibehaltung des Hangs, auf dem das Gebäude steht, minimiert, scheint die Natur gemütlich in sein Inneres zu gleiten und sich dort zu installieren.

Doelstelling van het programma is het creëren van multifunctionele ruimtes in een gebouw dat wortel schiet in het omringende bos. Door het minimaliseren van de voetafdruk op de omgeving, het gebruik van autochtone materialen en het vermijden van het kappen van bomen of van het wijzigen van de helling waarop het gebouw staat, lijkt te natuur binnen te glippen en zich comfortabel in het interieur te nestelen.

El objetivo del programa es crear espacios multifuncionales en un edificio que eche raíces en el bosque que lo rodea. Al minimizar su huella sobre el entorno –utilizando materiales autóctonos o evitando talar árboles o modificar la pendiente en la que el edificio se asienta–, la naturaleza parece deslizarse e instalarse cómodamente en su interior.

L'obiettivo del programma consiste nel creare spazi multifunzione in un edificio che affondi le proprie radici nel bosco che lo circonda. Riducendo al minimo l'impronta ambientale tramite l'uso di materiali locali o evitando il taglio di alberi o l'alterazione del dislivello su cui poggia la struttura, la natura sembra scivolare e inserirsi comodamente al suo interno.

O objectivo do programa é criar espaços multifuncionais num edifício que tenha raízes no bosque que o rodeia. Ao minimizar a sua marca sobre o ambiente – utilizando materiais autóctones ou evitando derrubar árvores ou modificar a encosta sobre a qual o edifício assenta –, a natureza parece deslizar e instalar-se comodamente no seu interior.

Programmets mål är att skapa multifunktionella utrymmen i en byggnad som slår rot i den omgivande skogen. Genom att minimera spåren i omgivningen, med hjälp av lokala material eller genom att undvika att hugga ner träd eller modifiera sluttningen där byggnaden står, verkar naturen som glida in och slå sig till ro i dess inre.

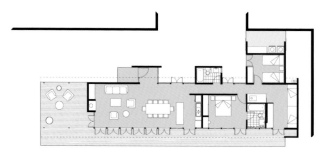

Floor plan

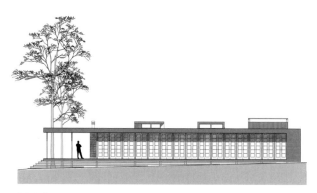

North elevation

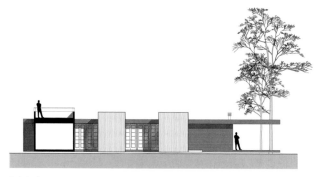

South elevation

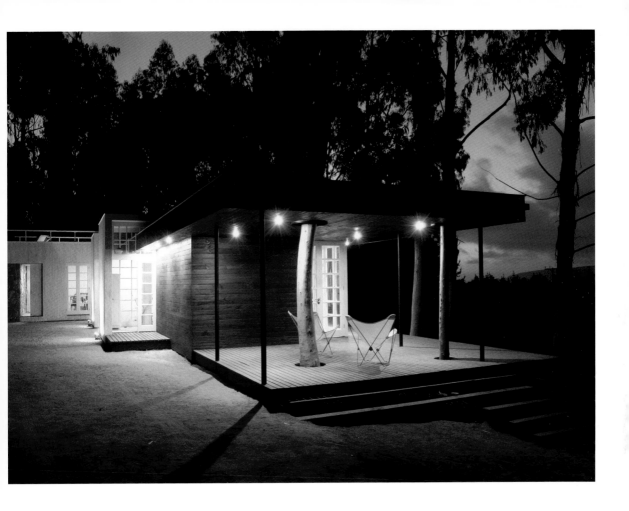

BERGMAN-WERNTOFT HOUSE

Johan Sundberg
Ljunghusen, Sweden
© Henrik Magnusson

The building embraces a conservatory in the shape of an atrium. Around it, a permeable glass membrane with sliding doors and windows, invites nature into the interior. The roof, pierced with light wells, comprises sheets of plywood that taper towards the patio. The exterior walls are lined with Siberian larch.

L'édifice comporte un jardin d'hiver façon atrium. Autour de celui-ci, une membrane en verre perméable, dotée de portes et de fenêtres coulissantes, invite la nature à entrer. Le toit, équipé de puits de lumière, comporte des planches en contreplaqué qui se resserrent vers la cour. Les murs extérieurs sont recouverts de cèdre sibérien.

Das Gebäude rahmt einen Wintergarten im Stil eines Atriums ein. Darum herum lädt eine durchlässige Glasmembrane mit Schiebetüren und -fenstern die Natur zum Eintritt ein. Die mit Lichtschächten durchbrochene Decke besteht aus furnierten Holzschichten, die bis zum Innenhof hin schmäler werden. Die Außenwände sind mit sibirischer Lärche verkleidet.

Het gebouw is tot stand gekomen rond een wintertuin in de vorm van een voorhof. Rondom nodigt een lichtdoorlatend glazen membraan met schuiframen en -deuren, de natuur uit om binnen te komen. Het dak met lichtkokers bestaat uit houten beplating die in de richting van de patio smaller worden. De buitenmuren zijn bekleed met Siberische lariks.

El edificio se abraza a un jardín de invierno a modo de atrio. En torno a él, una membrana de cristal permeable, con puertas y ventanas correderas, invita a la naturaleza a entrar. El techo, aguijoneado por pozos de luz, comprende láminas de madera enchapada que se estrechan hacia el patio. Las paredes exteriores están forradas de alerce siberiano.

L'edificio abbraccia un giardino d'inverno creando una sorta di cortile. Intorno a questo una membrana di vetro permeabile, con porte e finestre scorrevoli, invita la natura a entrare. Il soffitto, intervallato da punti di luce, comprende lastre di legno rivestito che si stringono verso il cortile. Le pareti esterne sono ricoperte di larice siberiano.

O edifício abraça-se a um jardim de inverno a jeitos de átrio. À sua volta, uma membrana de vidro permeável, com portas e janelas deslizantes, convida a natureza a entrar. O tecto, salpicado por poços de luz, compreende lâminas de madeira coberta por chapa que se estreitam na direcção do pátio. As paredes exteriores estão forradas de alerce siberiano.

Byggnaden omsluter en vinterträdgård som atrium. Runt den finns ett membran av permeabelt glas, med skjutdörrar och skjutbara fönster som bjuder in naturen. Taket, genomborrat av ljusbrunnar, består av plywoodplattor som sträcker sig mot innergården. Ytterväggarna är klädda med sibirisk lärk.

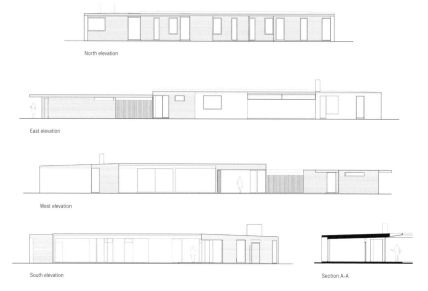

North elevation

East elevation

West elevation

South elevation

Section A-A

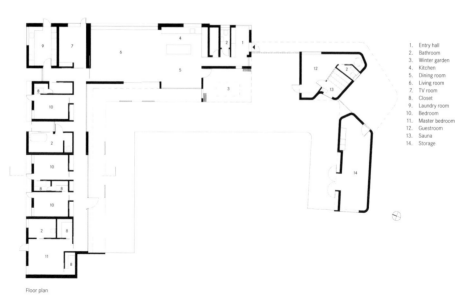

Floor plan

1. Entry hall
2. Bathroom
3. Winter garden
4. Kitchen
5. Dining room
6. Living room
7. TV room
8. Closet
9. Laundry room
10. Bedroom
11. Master bedroom
12. Guestroom
13. Sauna
14. Storage

SUMMERHOUSE IN **JØRLUNDE**

Dorte Mandrup Architects ApS
Jørlunde, Denmark
© Torben Eskerod

A concrete pillar brace allows the house to bridge the slight slope. Its open, rectangular plan, with its space organized around a central lobby atrium, blurs the boundaries between the interior and exterior space. Successive, peripherally arranged cloth screens filter the landscape, opening the house onto or inhibiting it.

Une rangée de piliers en béton permet à la maison de contrer la légère pente. Son plan ouvert rectangulaire, avec un espace organisé autour d'un vestibule central, définit les limites entre les zones intérieure et extérieure. Disposés de façon périphérique, des pans de tissu successifs laissent filtrer le paysage et ouvrent ainsi la maison sur celui-ci tout en la gardant dissimulée.

Ein Korsett aus Betonsäulen ermöglicht es dem Haus, den leichten Hang zu überwinden. Sein offener rechteckiger Grundriss mit dem um ein Atrium - Zentralflur herum organisierten Raum verwischt die Grenzen zwischen Innen- und Außenraum. Die auf der Kontur angeordneten aufeinanderfolgenden Stoffleinwände filtern die Landschaft, indem sie ihr das Haus öffnen oder es ihr enthalten.

Dankzij een korset van betonnen pilaren kan het huis de lichte helling overbruggen. Het rechthoekige open grondvlak, met een ruimte die georganiseerd is rond een centraal voorhof, doet de grens tussen binnen en buiten vervagen. Stoffen schermen langs de gehele omtrek filteren het landschap door het huis te openen of juist te verbergen.

Un corsé de pilares de cemento permite a la casa salvar la ligera pendiente. Su planta rectangular abierta, con su espacio organizado en torno a un atrio-distribuidor central, desdibuja los límites entre el espacio interior y exterior. Dispuestas perimetralmente, sucesivas pantallas de tela filtran el paisaje, abriendo la casa a él o inhibiéndola.

Una serie di pilastri in cemento consente alla casa di poggiare sul leggero dislivello. La pianta rettangolare aperta, con uno spazio organizzato intorno a un atrio-disimpegno centrale, confonde i limiti tra spazio interno ed esterno. Disposti perimetralmente, vari pannelli di tela filtrano il paesaggio, aprendo la casa a questo o isolandola da esso.

Um cinta de pilares de cimento permite à casa salvar a leve encosta. A sua planta rectangular aberta, com o seu espaço organizado em torno a um átrio-distribuidor central, apaga os limites entre o espaço interior e exterior. Dispostas ao longo do perímetro, sucessivas telas de tecido filtram a paisagem, abrindo a casa para esta ou tampando-a.

Ett bälte av betongpelare tillåter huset att kompensera för den svaga sluttningen. Det öppna, rektangulära våningsplanet med sin rumsfördelning kring ett centralt atrium suddar ut gränserna mellan interiör och exteriör. Genom successiva skärmar av tyg, perifert anordnade, filtreras landskapet och öppnar upp huset utåt eller undertrycker det.

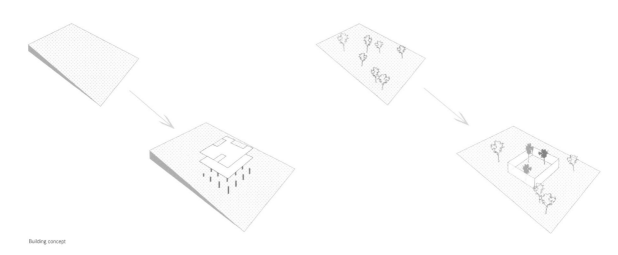

Building concept

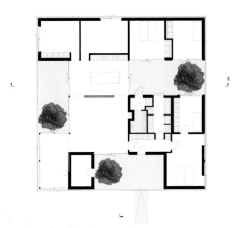

Floor plan

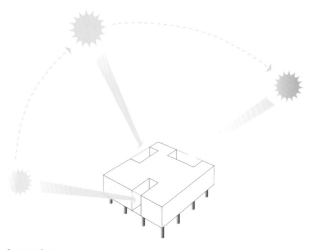

Sun exposure diagram

Building section

Building section

VERMONT CABIN

Resolution: 4 Architecture
Jamaica, VT, USA
© Resolution: 4 Architecture

The building is a modular composition in L-shape, with the communal spaces arranged vertically and the rest areas in the basement. Among them, facing west to capture sunlight, there is a terrace with a hearth. Inside, the abundant wood and, outside, the Corten Kynar® corrugated metal shell, relieve the harsh climate of Vermont.

Ce bâtiment est une composition modulable en forme de « L », avec les espaces communs sur l'axe vertical et le reste sur la base. Un porche est situé face à l'ouest, pour capter la lumière du soleil, et dispose d'une cheminée au sol. L'abondance du bois à l'intérieur et la toiture en tôle ondulée Corten Kynar® à l'extérieur atténuent le climat rude du Vermont.

Das Gebäude ist eine modulare Zusammenstellung in "L"-Form mit gemeinsamen Räumen auf der Vertikalen und dem restlichen Teil im Unterteil. Dazwischen, mit Blick in dem Westen, um das Sonnenlicht einzufangen, ist eine Terrasse mit Grillanlage angeordnet. Im Inneren mildern das reichhaltige Holz und außen das Dach aus Corten Kynar®metall das strenge Klima Vermonts.

Het gebouw is een L-vormige modulaire compositie met de gemeenschappelijke ruimtes in de verticale as en de overige in de basis. Daaronder ligt, op het westen om zonlicht te vangen, een overdekte galerij met barbecue. Het strenge klimaat van Vermont wordt binnen verlicht door veel hout en buiten door de kap van Corten Kynar® golfmetaal.

El edificio es una composición modular en forma de L con los espacios comunales en la vertical y el resto, en la base. Entre ellos, mirando al oeste para captar la luz solar, se dispone una terraza con fuego a tierra. En el interior, la abundante madera y, fuera, la cobertura de metal ondulado Corten Kynar® alivian el rigor del clima de Vermont.

L'edificio è una composizione modulare a forma di L con gli spazi comuni nella verticale e il resto nella base. Tra questi, guardando a ovest per catturare la luce del sole, troviamo un porticato con barbecue. All'interno l'uso abbondante di legno e fuori la copertura in metallo ondulato Corten Kynar® isolano dal rigido clima del Vermont.

O edifício é uma composição modular em forma de L com os espaços comuns na vertical e o resto, na base. Entre eles, orientada a oeste para captar a luz solar, encontra-se um alpendre com barbecue. No interior, a abundante madeira e, fora, a cobertura de metal ondulado Corten Kynar®, aliviam o rigor do clima de Vermont.

Byggnaden är en komposition i L-form med gemensamma utrymmen vertikalt och övriga utrymmen i underdelen. Bland annat finns en hemtrevlig veranda som vetter mot väster för att fånga upp solens strålar. Inomhus finns rikligt med trä och utomhus väggar av Corten Kynar®-korrugerad metall som avhjälper det stränga klimatet i Vermont.

Floor plan

NEAL CREEK RETREAT

Paul McKean Architecture
Hood River, OR, USA
© Paul McKean Architecture

Suspended over the forest, the house is like a lookout over the nearby creek. Its elevation, more than a whim, is a structural solution that prevents flooding and fires. The free space houses a central courtyard and storage areas. A green roof cools the interior of the house and reduces its footprint on the landscape.

Suspendue au-dessus du bois, la maison ressemble à un belvédère donnant sur le ruisseau voisin. Son élévation, plus qu'un simple caprice, constitue une solution structurelle contre les inondations et incendies. L'espace ainsi libéré héberge une cour et des zones de stockage. La toiture végétale permet de rafraîchir l'intérieur de la maison qui se confond davantage avec le paysage.

Das Haus hängt über dem Wald und sieht wie ein Aussichtsturm über den naheliegenden Bach aus. Seine hohe Lage ist kein Zufall, sondern eine strukturelle Lösung, die es vor Überschwemmungen und Bränden schützt. Der freigeräumte Bereich umfasst einen Innenhof und Lagerbereiche. Ein Pflanzdach kühlt den Innenraum des Hauses und verwischt seine Spur in der Spur in der Landschaft.

Het huis, dat boven het bos lijkt te hangen, vormt een uitkijkpunt over de nabijgelegen beek. De verhoogde ligging is, meer dan een gril, een structurele oplossing ter bescherming tegen overstromingen en brand. De vrijgekomen ruimte wordt gebruikt als patio en opslagruimte. Een plantendak koelt het interieur en vermindert de voetafdruk daarvan op het landschap.

Suspendida sobre el bosque, la casa parece un mirador sobre el cercano arroyo. Su elevación, más que un capricho, es una solución estructural que la protege de inundaciones e incendios. El espacio liberado aloja un patio y zonas de almacenaje. Una cubierta vegetal refrigera el interior de la casa y diluye su huella sobre el paisaje.

Sospesa sul bosco, la casa sembra un belvedere da cui ammirare il vicino ruscello. La sua particolare altezza, più che un capriccio è una soluzione strutturale che la salvaguarda da inondazioni e incendi. Lo spazio liberato dalla vegetazione ospita un cortile e alcune aree di contenimento. Un manto vegetale rinfresca gli interni della casa e diluisce l'impatto sul paesaggio.

Suspensa sobre o bosque, a casa parece um miradouro sobre o próximo ribeiro. A sua elevação, mais que um capricho, é uma solução estrutural que a protege de inundações e incêndios. O espaço libertado aloja um pátio e zonas de arrecadação. Uma cobertura vegetal refrigera o interior da casa e dilui a sua presença na paisagem.

Huset svävar över skogen och verkar som en utsiktsplats över den närliggande bäcken. Höjden är mer än en nyck, det är en lösning som skyddar mot översvämningar och bränder. Det fria utrymmet ger rum åt en patio samt förvaringsutrymme. Ett hölje av växtlighet håller husets inre svalt och sätter sin prägel på landskapet.

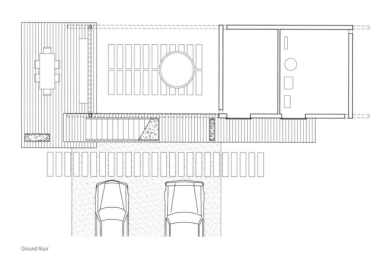

Ground floor

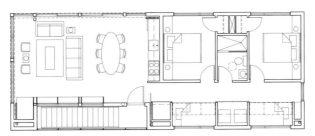

Second floor

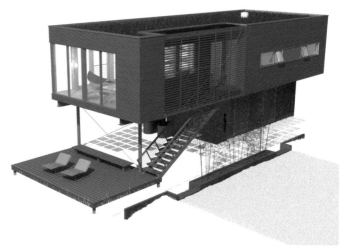

Axonometric view

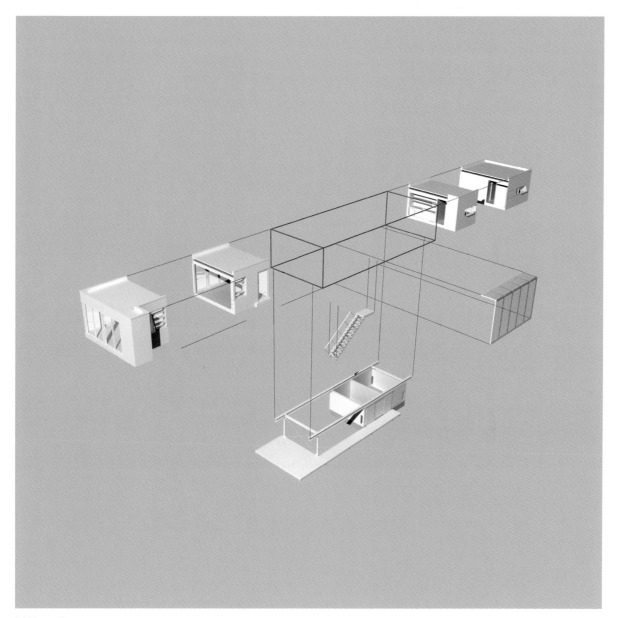

Exploded axonometric

BLUFF HOUSE

Bruns Architecture
Baraboo, WI, USA
© Bruns Architecture

Two main walls enclose a series of interlocking volumes. One of them separates private access from public access: both meet in a common hallway where there is a living room, kitchen and dining room. The cedar cladding of the walls relieves the enormity of the structure and reintegrates the building into the environment.

Deux murs porteurs renferment une série de volumes entrelacés. L'un d'eux sépare l'accès public de l'accès privé, qui convergent tous deux vers un vestibule commun où se trouvent la pièce à vivre, la cuisine et la salle à manger. Le revêtement en cèdre des cloisons atténue l'aspect massif de la structure et permet une meilleure intégration du bâtiment dans son environnement.

Zwei tragende Wände schließen eine Reihe untereinander verbundener Volumina ein. Eine der Wände trennt den öffentlichen vom privaten Bereich, wobei beide in einem gemeinsamen Flur zusammenfließen, wo sich Wohnzimmer, Küche und Esszimmer befinden. Die Zedernholzverkleidung der Zwischenwände lockert das Massive der Struktur auf und bringt das Gebäude wieder in sein Umfeld zurück.

Twee draagmuren sluiten een serie met elkaar verweven volumes in. Een daarvan scheidt de publiekelijk toegankelijke delen af van de privé-vertrekken: beide komen uit in een gemeenschappelijke vestibule waar zich de zitkamer, keuken en eetkamer bevinden. De cederhouten bekleding van de scheidingswanden maakt de massiefheid van de structuur lichter en doet het gebouw opnieuw in de omgeving integreren.

Dos paredes maestras encierran una serie de volúmenes entrelazados. Una de ellas separa el acceso público del privado: ambos convergen en un vestíbulo común donde se hayan la sala de estar, la cocina y el comedor. El revestimiento de cedro de los tabiques alivia la masividad de la estructura y reintegra el edificio al entorno.

Due pareti maestre racchiudono una serie di volumi interconnessi. Una di queste separa l'accesso pubblico da quello privato: entrambi convergono in un atrio comune dove si sviluppano salotto, cucina e tinello. Il rivestimento in cedro delle pareti divisorie alleggerisce la struttura e reintegra l'edificio nel contesto circostante.

Duas paredes-mestras encerram uma série de volumes entrelaçados. Um delas separa o acesso público do privado: ambos convergem num vestibulo comum onde se encontram a sala de estar, a cozinha e a sala de jantar. O revestimento de cedro dos tabiques alivia o maciço da estrutura e reintegra o edificio no ambiente.

Två huvudväggar omsluter en rad samverkande kroppar. En av dem separerar den privata ingången från allmänhetens, båda konvergerar i en gemensam hall där man finner vardagsrum, kök och matsal. Mellanväggarna beklädda med cederträ lättar upp det massiva i strukturen och innesluter byggnaden i omgivningen.

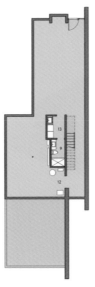

Lower floor

Main floor

1. Entry walk
2. Entry
3. Circulation hall
4. Kitchen
5. Dining room
6. Living room
7. Bedroom
8. Walk-in closet
9. Bathroom
10. Garage
11. Deck
12. Mechanical room
13. Laundry

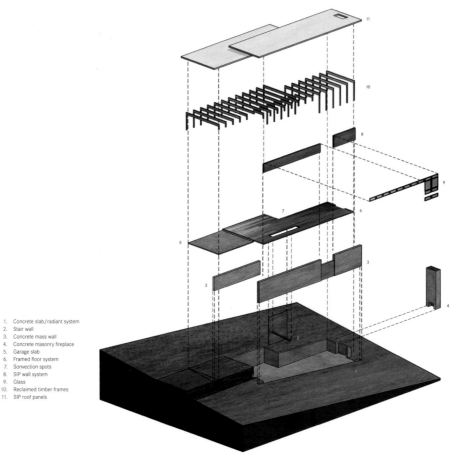

1. Concrete slab/radiant system
2. Stair wall
3. Concrete mass wall
4. Concrete masonry fireplace
5. Garage slab
6. Framed floor system
7. Sonvection spots
8. SIP wall system
9. Glass
10. Reclaimed timber frames
11. SIP roof panels

Exploded axonometric

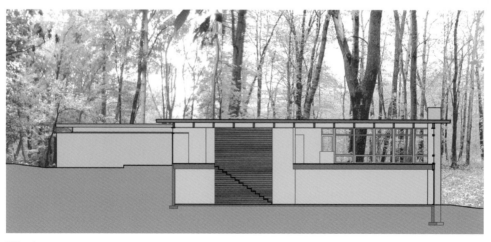

Building section

CASA **G**

Gudmundur Jonsson Arkitektkontor
Iceland
© Bragi Thor Josefsson

The structure of the house adapts to its environment. Its northern entrance and the curved plane project it to the south, opening it to the sea. A sloping wooden wall creates a corridor between sea and mountains only interrupted by a bay window, facing west, framing the glaciers. Inside, the staircase and floor share an Icelandic basalt covering.

La structure de la maison l'intègre dans son environnement. Son entrée nord et son plan courbe la projettent vers le sud, l'ouvrant sur la mer. Un mur incliné en bois crée un couloir entre la mer et la montagne, seulement interrompu par une fenêtre qui, orientée à l'ouest, encadre les glaciers. À l'intérieur, les escaliers et le sol partagent un revêtement en basalte islandais.

Der Aufbau des Hauses passt es seine Umgebung an. Sein Nordeingang und sein gewundener Entwurf orientieren es zum Süden hin, indem sie es zum Meer hin öffnen. Eine geneigte Holzmauer bildet einen Weg zwischen Meer und Berg, der nur durch ein nach Westen ausgerichtetes Fenster - als Rahmen für die Gletscher - unterbrochen wird. Innerhalb des Hauses teilen sich Treppe und Boden einen Belag aus isländischem Basalt.

De structuur van de woning zorgt ervoor dat zij zich aan de omgeving aanpast. De ingang aan de noordzijde en het gebogen vlak zijn naar zuiden gericht en stellen het huis open naar de zee. Een schuine, houten muur creëert een gang tussen de zee en de bergen en wordt alleen onderbroken door een groot raam op het westen, dat de gletsjers inlijst. Van binnen zijn zowel de trap als de vloer bekleed met IJslands basalt.

La estructura de la casa la amolda a su entorno. Su entrada norte y su plano curvo la proyectan al sur, abriéndola al mar. Un muro inclinado de madera crea un pasillo entre mar y montaña sólo interrumpido por un ventanal que, orientado al oeste, enmarca los glaciares. Dentro, la escalera y el suelo comparten una cobertura de basalto islandés.

La struttura della casa la armonizza con il contesto circostante. L'ingresso nord e il piano curvo la proiettano a sud, con apertura verso il mare. Un muro inclinato in legno crea un corridoio tra mare e montagna, interrotto solo da un finestrone che, orientato verso ovest, incornicia i ghiacciai. All'interno, la scala e il pavimento condividono una copertura in basalto islandese.

A estrutura da casa adapta-se ao seu ambiente. A sua entrada norte e a planta curva projectam-na para sul, abrindo-a para o mar. Uma parede de madeira inclinada cria um corredor entre mar e montanhas apenas interrompida por uma janela de sacada, virada para oeste, emoldurando os glaciares. No interior, as escadas e o pavimento partilham basalto islandês.

Husets struktur passar in i omgivningen. Dess norra entré och den böjda formen riktar huset söderut och öppnar upp det mot havet. En sluttande trävägg skapar en gång mellan hav och berg som endast avbryts av ett större fönster mot väster, där glaciärerna ramas in. Inomhus täcks trappa och golv av basalt från Island.

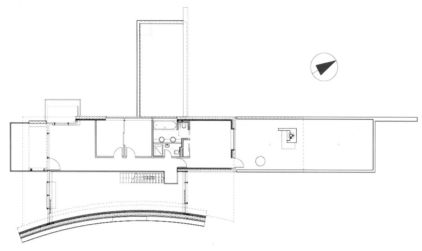

Second floor

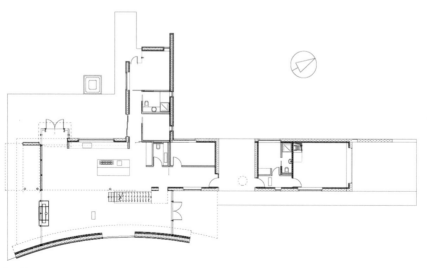

Ground floor

PRIVATE HOUSE IN **SIGULDA**

ARHIS
Sigulda, Latvia
© Indrikis Sturmanis and Mikelis Putrams

The small slope on the banks of the river Gauja where the building rests was excavated and filled in once finished. The orthogonal geometry of its structure, of radical horizontality, governs its whimsical volume and spatial composition. The warmth and lightness of the wood satisfy the strength of its naked structure.

Le petit versant bordant le fleuve de la Gauja, sur lequel se trouve l'édifice, a été creusé puis rempli une fois celui-ci terminé. La géométrie octogonale de sa structure, radicalement horizontale, régit sa volumétrie capricieuse et sa composition spatiale. La chaleur et la légèreté du bois atténuent la robustesse de sa structure dénudée.

Der kleine Hang am Ufer des Gauja-Flusses, in den das Haus eingesetzt wurde, wurde ausgeschachtet und danach wieder aufgefüllt. Die rechteckige Geometrie der Struktur mit strenger Horizontalität bestimmt die kapriziöse Volumetrie und räumliche Zusammenstellung des Hauses. Wärme und Leichtigkeit des Holzes lindern die optische Wirkung seiner blanken Struktur.

De kleine berghelling aan de oevers van de rivier de Gauja, waar dit gebouw is ingepast, is uitgegraven en na de bouw weer opgevuld. De rechthoekige geometrie van de structuur, de radicale horizontaliteit, regelt de grillige volumetrie en ruimtelijke indeling. Het warme en lichte hout verzacht de stelligheid van de naakte structuur.

La pequeña ladera que orilla al río Gauja en la que el edificio está encajado fue excavada y se rellenó una vez acabado éste. La geometría ortogonal de su estructura, de radical horizontalidad, rige su caprichosa volumetría y composición espacial. La calidez y la ligereza de la madera aplacan la contundencia de su estructura desnuda.

Il piccolo dislivello che costeggia il fiume Gauja, sul quale si inserisce l'edificio, è stato scavato per poi essere nuovamente riempito alla fine dei lavori. La geometria ortogonale della struttura, radicalmente orizzontale, ne domina la capricciosa volumetria e composizione spaziale. Il calore e la leggerezza del legno smorzano la struttura spoglia e contundente.

A pequena ladeira que faz margem ao rio Gauja na qual o edifício está encaixado foi escavada e preenchida uma vez acabado este. A geometria ortogonal da sua estrutura, de radical horizontalidade, rege a sua caprichosa volumetria e composição espacial. A calidez e leveza da madeira suavizam a contundência da sua estrutura despida.

Den lilla backen mot floden Gauja där byggnaden ligger grävdes ut och fylldes sedan när bygget var klart. Stommens vinkelräta geometri, radikalt horisontell, reglerar dess nyckfulla rymd och spatiala komposition. Värmen och lättheten i träet dämpar styrkan i den nakna strukturen.

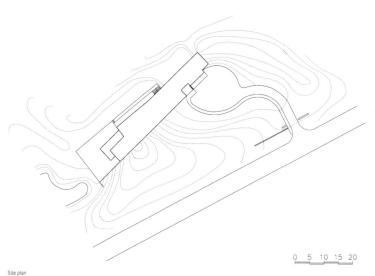

Site plan

0 5 10 15 20

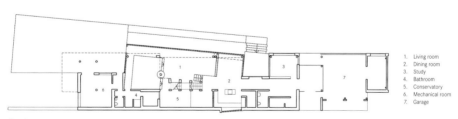

Floor plan

1. Living room
2. Dining room
3. Study
4. Bathroom
5. Conservatory
6. Mechanical room
7. Garage

Building section

OLNICK SPANU HOUSE

Estudio Alberto Campo Baeza
Garrison, NY, USA
© Javier Callejas, Hisao Suzuki, Estudio Campo Alberto Baeza

A sturdy platform with concrete walls covered with travertine sustains a glass box crowned with a lightweight roof whose weight supports ten steel cylindrical pillars. Above, the common areas and the ubiquitous landscape act as a stage. In the cement shelter, an Arte Povera lobby-gallery leads to the bedrooms and bathrooms.

Une plateforme, composée de murs solides en béton et d'une toiture en travertin, soutient un bloc en verre couronné d'un toit léger dont le poids est supporté par dix piliers cylindriques en acier. En haut, se trouvent les espaces communs, avec le paysage omniprésent pour décor. L'abri en béton héberge quant à lui un vestibule-galerie d'art Povera conduisant aux chambres et salles de bains.

Eine Plattform mit dicken Betonwänden und Travertindach trägt einen Glaskasten, der von einer leichten Decke gekrönt ist, dessen wiederum Gewicht zehn runde Stahlsäulen tragen. Oben bilden die gemeinsamen Bereiche und die allgegenwärtige Landschaft die Inszenierung. Im Betonbunker führt eine Arte Povera Diele / Galerie zu den Schlafzimmern und Bädern.

Een platform van robuuste betonnen muren met een travertijnen dak draagt een glazen kast met een licht dak waarvan het gewicht gedragen wordt door tien cilindervormige stalen pilaren. Boven bevinden zich de gemeenschappelijke zones en het omnipresente landschap is als een mise-en-scène. In het betonnen toevluchtsoord leidt een vestibule en galerij van Arte Povera naar de slaapkamers en badkamers.

Una plataforma de recias paredes de hormigón con cubierta de travertino sostiene una caja de cristal coronada por un ligero techo cuyo peso soportan diez pilares cilíndricos de acero. Arriba, las zonas comunes y el ubicuo paisaje como puesta en escena. En el refugio de cemento, un vestíbulo-galería de *arte povera* conduce a los dormitorios y a los baños.

Una piattaforma con robuste pareti di cemento e rivestimento di travertino sostiene una struttura in vetro sovrastata da un tetto leggero il cui peso è sostenuto da dieci piloni cilindrici di acciaio. Nella parte alta troviamo le zone comuni e l'onnipresente paesaggio. Nel rifugio di cemento, un corridoio-galleria di Arte Povera porta alle camere e ai bagni.

Uma plataforma de grossas paredes de betão com cobertura de travertino sustém uma caixa de vidro coroada por um leve tecto cujo peso é suportado por dez pilares cilíndricos de aço. Em cima, as zonas comuns e a omnipresente paisagem como colocada em encenação. No refúgio de cimento, um vestíbulo-sala de Arte Pobre conduz aos quartos e casas de banho.

En plattform med robusta betongväggar täckta med travertinsten bär upp en låda av glas, med ett lätt tak högst upp, vars tyngd stöttas av tio cylindriska stål. Där uppe finns gemensamma utrymmen och det allestädes närvarande landskapet som om det vore iscensatt. I skydd av cementen leder en hall/Arte Povera-galleri till sovrum och badrum.

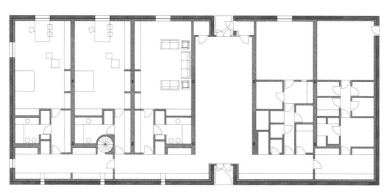

Basement – cave

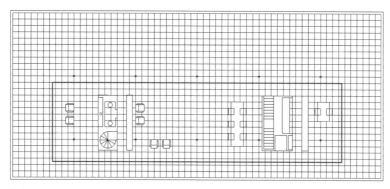

Glass box plan

Building section

KOM HOUSE IN **ORANJEWOUD**

Borren Staalenhoef Architecten
Oranjewould, The Netherlands
© Pieter Kers, Amsterdam

The main idea of the design was to integrate architecture and landscape. The sand excavated for the foundations and a new pond give continuity to the forest that surrounds the building. Nine steel beams sustain a concrete wall that shields the winds and declutters the main façade of obstacles that interfere with the landscape.

L'idée centrale du projet était d'intégrer l'architecture au paysage. Le sable issu des fondations et le nouveau bassin créent une continuité avec l'ambiance forestière qui encadre le bâtiment. Neuf colonnes en acier soutiennent un mur de béton qui assure une protection contre le vent et dégage la façade principale de tout obstacle pouvant interférer avec le paysage.

Die Grundidee des Entwurfs lautete, Architektur und Landschaft zu integrieren. Der vom Fundament ausgegrabene Sand und ein neuer Teich bilden die Fortsetzung des Waldgebiets, das das Gebäude umgibt. Neun Stahlsäulen tragen eine Betonwand, die vor Wind schützt und die Hauptfassade von Hindernissen frei hält, die sich auf die Landschaft auswirken.

De vorm van het originele eeuwenoude huis met zijn smalle ramen is behouden en alleen de opvallende beglaasde veranda en de sobere houten bekleding —askleurig, net als de teer op de vissersboten die hier weleer voor anker gingen– maken dat het opvalt tussen de aangrenzende gebouwen met hun atavistisch torentjes en decoratieve puntgevels.

La idea cardinal del diseño era integrar arquitectura y paisaje. La arena excavada de los cimientos y un nuevo estanque dan continuidad al tejido forestal que rodea al inmueble. Nueve columnas de acero sostienen una pared de hormigón que apantalla los vientos y despeja la fachada principal de obstáculos que interfieran en el paisaje.

L'idea alla base del progetto era quella di integrare architettura e paesaggio. La sabbia scavata dalle fondamenta e un nuovo stagno danno continuità al tessuto forestale che circonda l'edificio. Nove colonne di acciaio sostengono una parete in cemento armato che ripara dai venti e libera la facciata principale da qualsiasi ostacolo che interferisca con il paesaggio.

A ideia cardinal do desenho era integrar arquitectura e paisagem. A areia escavada das fundações e um novo tanque dão continuidade ao tecido florestal que rodeia o imóvel. Nove colunas de aço sustentam uma parede de betão que protege dos ventos e esvazia a fachada principal de obstáculos que interferem na paisagem.

Designens grundidé var att integrera arkitektur och landskap. Sanden som grävdes ut från grunden och den nya dammen ger kontinuitet till skogsvävnaden som omger byggnaden. Nio stålbalkar stöder en betongvägg som ger vindskydd och håller huvudväggen ren från störande hinder i landskapet.

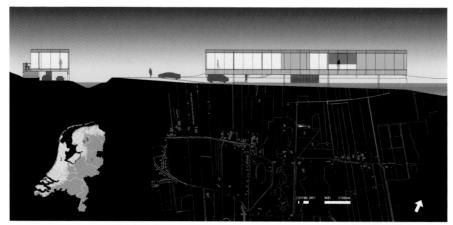

Location map, west elevation and south elevation

1. Above sea level
2. Under sea level
3. Location
4. Former royal estate
5. Forest
6. Pond
7. Field

Floor plan, east elevation and longitudinal section

1. Entrance
2. Living room
3. Study
4. Bedroom
5. Master bedroom
6. Covered terrace
7. Parking

...
et celui de la na...

Das Gebäude stellt einen einfachen Entwurf da.,
Die vorhandene Stahlstruktur definiert den Wohnbereich: Glass...
den häuslichen Bereich. Weiter weg zeichnet das nackte Skelett Vorhallen ode...
Übergang zwischen der Welt der Menschen und der Natur.

Het gebouw krijgt vorm in een eenvoudig ontwerp dat aanleiding is voor een complexe
ruimtelijke indeling. De stalen structuur, die vooraf al bestond, definieert de woonsfeer:
de glazen, houten en stenen schermen omringen het leefgedeelte; verder weg tekent het
naakte skelet arcades of voorhoven, als overgang tussen de menselijke wereld en de natuur.

El edificio plasma un diseño sencillo que da pie a una compleja distribución espacial.
La estructura de acero preexistente define el ámbito residencial: las pantallas de cristal,
madera y piedra cercan el espacio doméstico; más allá, el esqueleto desnudo dibuja porches
o atrios a modo de transición entre el mundo humano y la naturaleza.

L'edificio riflette un progetto semplice che dà vita a una complessa distribuzione spaziale.
La struttura in acciaio preesistente definisce il contesto residenziale: i pannelli in vetro, legno
e pietra circoscrivono lo spazio domestico; più in là, lo scheletro nudo disegna porticati o atri
creando spazi di transizione tra il mondo umano e la natura.

O edifício espelha um desenho simples que dá origem a uma complexa distribuição espacial.
A estrutura de aço preexistente define o âmbito residencial: as telas de vidro, madeira e pedra
cercam o espaço doméstico; mais além, a estrutura despida desenha alpendres e átrios que
funcionam como transição entre o mundo humano e a natureza.

Byggnaden förkroppsligar en enkel design som ger upphov till en komplex rumsutspridning.
Den befintliga stålkonstruktionen definierar bostadsutrymmet. Skärmarna av glas, trä och sten
omger hemmet. Bortom detta skissas verandor eller atrium fram av den nakna stommen, som
övergångar mellan människa och natur.

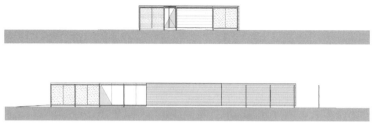

East and north elevations

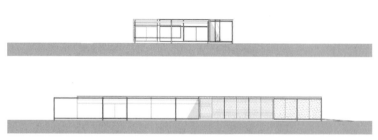

West and south elevations

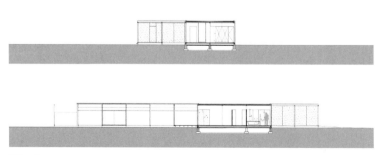

Building sections

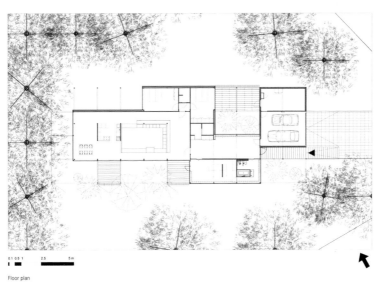

Floor plan

DIRECTORY/REPERTOIRE

Altius Architecture
Toronto, Canada
http://altius.net

Anna Noguera
Barcelona, Spain
http://annanoguera.com/

ARHIS
Riga, Latvia
www.arhis.lv

ARTechnic Architects
Tokyo, Japan
www.artechnic.jp

Arteks Arquitectura
Andorra la Vella, Andorra
www.arteksarquitectura.com

Bark Design Architects
Noosa Heads, Australia
www.barkdesign.com.au

Bjarne Mastenbroek/SeARCH, Christian Müller/CMA
Amsterdam / Rotterdam, The Netherlands
www.search.nl/www.christian-muller.com

Borja García, Sergio García-Gasco, Jorge Cortés
Valencia, Spain
www.borjagarcia.es

Borren Staalenhoef Architecten
Leeuwarden, The Netherlands
www.borrenstaalenhoef.com

Bruns Architecture
Baraboo, WI, USA
www.brunsarchitecture.com

BURO II & ARCHI+I
Brussels, Belgium
www.buro2.be

CCS Architecture
San Francisco, CA / New York, NY, USA
www.ccs-architecture.com

Christian Leibenger
Barcelona, Spain
xavi_rdz@hotmail.com

David Salmela
Duluth, MN, USA
http://salmelaarchitect.com

David Vandervort Architects
Seattle, WA, USA
www.vandervort.com

DeForest Architects
Seattle, WA, USA
www.deforestarchitects.com

Dietrich + Untertrifaller Architekten
Bregenz / Vienna, Austria; St. Gallen, Switzerland
www.dietrich.untertrifaller.com

Dorte Mandrup Architects ApS
Copenhagen, Denmark
www.dortemandrup.dk

Ecospace
London, United Kingdom
www.candwarch.co.uk

Eduardo Cadaval, Clara Solà-Morales
Mexico City, Mexico
www.ca-so.com

Erik Ståhl
Jönköping, Sweden
es-acoopab@telia.com

Estudio Alberto Campo Baeza
Madrid, Spain
www.campobaeza.com

Felipe del Río, Federico Campino/OPA
Santiago, Chile
www.opa.cl

Florian Maurer/Allen + Maurer Architects Ltd.
Pentincton, Canada / Lana, Italy
www.allenmaurer.com

Gerold Wiederin
Vienna, Austria
arch.wiederin@netway.at

González Vergara Arquitectos (formerly F3 Arquitectos)
Santiago, Chile
www.gv-arquitectos.cl

Gudmundur Jonsson Arkitektkontor
Oslo, Norway
www.gudmundurjonsson.no

Jarmund/Vigsnæs
Oslo, Norway
www.jva.no

Johan Sundberg
Lund, Sweden
www.johansundberg.com

Marià Castelló
Formentera, Spain
www.m-ar.net

Mats Edlund, Henrietta Palmer, Matts Ingman
Stockholm, Sweden
matsedlund.henriettapalmer.se/www.mattsingman.se

Nick Willson Architects
London, United Kingdom
www.nickwillsonarchitects.com

NORD Architecture
Glasgow / London, United Kingdom
http://nordarchitecture.com

OBRA Architects
New York, NY, USA / Beijing, China
www.obraarchitects.com

Pablo Fernández, Pablo Redondo
Madrid, Spain
www.arquipablos.com

Paul McKean Architecture
Portland, OR, USA
http://pmckean.com

Per Friberg Arkitektbyrå
Stockholm, Sweden

Pfeiffer Architekten
Berlin, Germany
www.pfeiffer-architekten.de

Pokorny Architekti
Bratislava, Slovakia
www.pokornyarchitekti.sk

Resolution: 4 Architecture
New York, NY, USA
http://re4a.com

Satoshi Okada
Tokyo, Japan
www.okada-archi.com

Shin Ohori, Setaro Aso/General Design
Tokyo, Japan
www.general-design.net

Signer Harris Architects
Boston, MA, USA
www.signerharris.com

Simon Winstanley Architects
Castle Douglas, United Kingdom
www.candwarch.co.uk

Turnbull Griffin Haesloop Architects
San Francisco, CA, USA
http://tgharchitects.com

UXUS
Amsterdam, The Netherlands / Napa, CA, USA
www.uxusdesign.com

ZeroEnergy Design
Boston, MA, USA
www.zeroenergy.com